Roads
from the
Ashes

*An Odyssey in Real Life
on the Virtual Frontier*

Roads
from the
Ashes

*An Odyssey in Real Life
on the Virtual Frontier*

by Megan Edwards

Trilogy Books
Pasadena, California

Cover Design: Joanne Stevens Art & Design

In order to protect privacy, some names of people and places have been changed.

RoadTrip America® and RoadTrip Report® are registered trademarks of O.D.C., Inc., a California corporation.

Author photo by Florence Photography, Altadena, CA.

Publisher's Cataloging in Publication

Edwards, Megan
      Roads from the ashes : an odyssey in real life
   on the virtual frontier / by Megan Edwards --
   1st ed.
      p. cm.
      ISBN: 1-891290-01-0

      1. Edwards, Megan--Journeys--United States.
   2. United States--Description and travel.
   3. United States--Social life and customs-1971-
   4. Automobile travel--United States.   5.
   Journalists--United States--Biography.   I.
   Title.

   E169.04.E39 1999   973.929

Library of Congress Catalog Card Number: 98-61898

This book, along with my heart, belongs to Mark

Together we dedicate it to our parents:

Margaret and Charles
Betty Lee and Spencer

✦ CONTENTS ✦

✦ ACKNOWLEDGMENTS ✦

People make the journey, and people have provided the substance of this book. Thanks are due to everyone whose lives have intertwined with ours on the road and online.

First and foremost, thanks to my husband, Mark Sedenquist, for his endless patience and unfailing support, and to Marvin the Road Dog, for sticking with us through thick and thin.

Thanks to our families, who have cheerfully supported us even when our goals exceeded what common sense allowed: Betty & Spencer Edwards, Margaret & Charles Sedenquist, Matt, Libby, Rachel, Eleanor & Margaret Brennesholtz, Robin, Jay, Patrick & Morgan Reidy, M'liss & Brady Edwards, Ray & Bruce Kristinson, Skye McPhail, Megan Graff, Don Huserau, Betty & Don Graff, Daniel, Lynette & Nicholas Sedenquist, Josh & Michelle Jacques, Diana Sedenquist, Alexandra, Bryant & Cader Duffy, and Ruth Hageman.

Thanks to all friends and angels who have sustained us with goodwill, fellowship and help in time of need: Larry Goldberg & Kathleen DiCiolla, Ivy Sun, Tom, Andrea & Alex Martin, Bob & Marjorie Miller, Pat & Logan Doyle, Phyllis & Dave Goddard, Deputy Phil Neumeyer, Mikki & Roger Pulse, Terry & Brad Thode, Toni & Bob Billetz, Jeff Cohen, Ron Zielaznicki, Kim Mctiernan, Doug, Nan & Lambert Semelveis, Gene Davies, Robert, Becky, Ryan & Jessica Lommel, Charlie, Barb, Katie & Mackenzie Brister, Ken Veronda, Manny Mendoza, Alan Frizzle, and the unknown driver of a glass delivery truck in Virginia Beach.

Without the knowledge, patience and expert care of mechanical and electronic wizards, not a single mile could have rolled under us, and all dreams of mobile Web publishing would have remained in the ether. Thanks to all whose talents made the unlikely possible, especially Wes Ferrari, Ron Gillentine, Don Bulen, Craig Fellows, Doug Grossman, David Cramer, Mike & Cathi McDade, Gene Rardon, Ron Nishioka, Mark Talmo, Daniel Harlow, Bob Klar, Bernard Uy, James Nesbitt, Daryl Cross, Roger Bush, John & Suzanne Burnett, Tidewater Mack, Bill & Bobbie Dunn, Dan Rutherford, Tom Freeman, Mark Helmlinger, Jon Barbieri, Robert Morse, Eric Davis, John Wilson, Kara Lakkees, Terry Fowler, and Jack Zeeman.

To all who have given so generously of their time, talent, resources and professional expertise, thank you: Carolyn and Bill Strong, Robin Salzer, Frank & Marlene Griffith, Emelita S.L. Bituin, Celinda Puelma, Ray & Beth Case, Dr. Barbara Kelly, Dr. Fred Rowe, Dr. Mahlon Chinn, Bill Nunnery, Evan Kent, Jim Rider, Pamela Kling, Dan Coates, Rick Parra, Rose Corona, Dr. George Sonneborn.

To Trilogy Books and Marge Wood, thanks for wisdom, patience, encouragement, talent and inspiration, and to Jim Laris, my unending appreciation for letting an untested writer use untested machinery to file stories from the boondocks. For encouragement and perpetual good cheer, thanks to Paula Johnson. For help with facts, history and geographical detail, thanks to Merle McClelland, Dave Schul, John Amanson, Robin Reidy, and the reference librarians of the Pasadena Public Library.

For professional excellence and support, thanks to Melissa & Bill Paule, Joanie Stevens, Gerry Casanova, Nadine Woloshin, Renee Baer, Brian Bailey, Susan Gibowicz, Peter Paris, Angie Cecil, Elisia Greiner, Steve & Liz Kapur, Elizabethe Kramer, Bill Schwab, Gary Chow, Mayrav Saar, Peter Serling, Florence Cole, Samantha Miller, Mort Arken, Bob Suter, Liz Miles, Dennis Fiely, John Pertzborn, Patricia Corrigan, Jeff Crilley, Suellen Knopick, Tracy Berry, and Marcella Gauthier.

For inspiration, suggestions, ideas, encouragement, friendship, and wonderful memories, thanks to Robert, Rebecca, Ryan and Jessica Lommel, Chuck Bausback, Art Holmes, David Kirby, Ray & Judy LaMadeleine, Craig Smith, Susan Howson, Ruth Alton, Kenyon King, Lisa Herron, Bruce and Joy Jones, Ellen Crawford, Larry Crain, Jerry Jinrich, Ray Starke, Bill MacGowan, Peter Richards, Ron Robertson, Joan & Jeff Stanford, John, Rosemary, Max & Claire Magee, Pat, Peggy and Tobi Whitten, Tim Viens, Karen Murray, Bill & Eleanor Bade, Dwain Robbins, Hants & Annie White, Evelyn & Jan Kok, Kent Horton, Father Keith Outlaw, George & Mary Regas, Frank & Janet Gortsema, Byron Porter, Carl Schwing & Tom Beletic, Bill Reading, Marty Slayton Churchwell, Randy & Ruthanne Perkins, Rev. Carol Shab, Tom Marvin & Marta Anton, Lew Zaharako, Ray Streblow, Ron & Angelita Schaaff, Susan Mosler, Fern & Don Myers, Leroy Powell Jr., Park Kerr, Angie Dean, Doug Davis, Jack & Alice Knight, Dianna May, Al Parker, Diane Hall, Tom & Carol Tucker, Lynn Bjorklund, James Rogers, Chris Northrup, Ed Czach, Sparky Cohen, Hobart Brown, Robert & Claire Kerr, Dave Robben, Ruth & Roy McAllister, Larry & Carol Rosenblum, Doug Gogel, Tammy Day, Heather Mauch, Steve Strangio, Peter Catanzaro, Bunny & Bonnie Gregory, Gary & Kathy Nickerson, Dennis & Corrine Vitolo, Larry & Judy McElwee, Joanne & John Ely, Kathy Hall, Sam Kloberdanz, Steven Shepard, Sandy Schulz, Jim & Louise Stivers, Miriam Pederson, Esler Johnson, Becky & Keith Deener, Norma Sotak, Claudia & Eric Chiasson, Mark Harmsen, Fred Worster, and Loyd Mayes.

There are more of you, many more. Mark and Marvin join me in thanking you all for the wonder and privilege of living in a home that circles the globe.

$\cdot$ 1 $\cdot$

Life's Ballast Lost

A Suitcase, An Arrowhead, and A Set of Red Underwear

You don't keep extra clothes when you live in 200 square feet. It's a question of being able to put your plate down when you eat dinner or owning an evening purse. I haven't owned an evening purse since 1993, and the one time I needed one since then, I found a perfectly good pearled specimen at a thrift store in New York. It cost a dollar, and I gave it to a bag lady in Grand Central Station after a dinner party at the Knickerbocker Club.

Okay, I confess. If you were to find yourself looking through my underwear box (yes, box— there aren't many drawers in motor homes), you'd find a red bra and pair of red panties at the bottom. They never move. I haven't worn them since before I owned an evening purse, but there they are. I can't throw them away. They're survivors.

That red underwear, one suitcase, one husband and one dog are the only things I have that antedate the fire that ended Phase One of my life. It arrived with perfect timing. I was 40 years old, and I'd just been wondering if this—a nice house in a nice neighborhood full of nice stuff— was all there was. Just like a jillion baby boomers on the exact cusp of middle age, I was sick of exercise videos and women's magazines and nylon stockings. I was having a hard time believing that the road to serenity lay in losing ten pounds, highlighting my hair, or giving my kitchen a country look.

And then, only a couple of months before I turned 41, Los Angeles caught on fire and didn't stop burning for seventeen days. My house was one of the first to go. One day, I had an answering machine and high heels and an eyelash curler. The next day, well, the next day things were different.

The fires were headline news for weeks, as Altadena, Laguna, and Malibu each hosted a conflagration bigger than the last. In dollars, a billion went up in smoke. Over 1,100 houses burned to the ground, and 4 people died. My loss seems minuscule in comparison: just one average middle class woman's stuff.

Yes, just stuff. That's all it was: high school yearbooks, photographs, wedding presents, diplomas, my grandmother's piano. I'd had ten minutes to pack ahead of the firestorm. I'd grabbed a suitcase. I'd grabbed—only God knows why— my red underwear.

I did take one other thing as I left the house. I paused in front of a cabinet filled with silver and wedding china and keepsakes. I opened the door and took out an Indian arrowhead I'd found in Wyoming on Mark's family's ranch.

I guess that's how you pack when you're off on a new life. You get ten minutes, and there's no second chance. I can't tell you why, as the flames roared nearer, I chose red underwear and an arrowhead that would have survived the fire anyway. I can only say this. Where I was headed, I was overpacked.

One Crystal Clear Autumn Morning

The fire started before dawn on October 27, 1993, and like most blazes near populated areas, it was set by a human, a homeless man named Andres Huang. He had hiked into the Altadena foothills during the night. He'd fallen asleep, and when he awoke before dawn, he was cold and shivering. He lit a little camp fire to warm himself up. It was a windy night, and the fire immediately got away from him. Frightened, he fled. Unable to see in the darkness, he fell over a cliff.

At 3:48 a.m., someone called Fire Station 66 at the foot of Eaton Canyon and reported "fire on the hillside." It was impossible to know it at the time, but that call mobilized the first unit of a force that would grow to include nearly three thousand firefighters from 62 different agencies, 200 fire engines, 15 water tenders, four bulldozers, eight helicopters, and fifteen airplanes.

Andres Huang was found, arrested and taken to a hospital. He was later charged with "reckless setting of a fire."

Mark and I were sleeping at home, a couple of ridge lines to the east. The telephone rang a little after four. It was Mark's mother, calling from her house, a couple more ridge lines to the east. She had awakened early and seen a tiny bright spot on the mountain. "There's a fire above Eaton Canyon," she said.

Mark and I got up and slid open the glass door that led from our bedroom to an outdoor patio. We could see a tiny, brilliant feather of flame on the dark slope.

We'd seen fires on the mountainside before. We'd grown up here. There were fires every year. Even though we lived in the hills, there were houses and streets between us and the native brush. Our house was nearly a hundred years old, nestled on a slope overlooking a reservoir that held a million gallons of water. The mountainside might burn, but our house? Unlikely, we thought. If the fire got close, we had the reservoir and a pump and a hose. On top of that, Mark used to be a fire fighter for the forest service. Whatever might happen, we'd be able to handle it.

"It's awfully windy," said Mark. And then we went back to bed.

We couldn't sleep. We got up, and I set to work addressing invitations in calligraphy for a friend. Mark went outside to work on the exhibit we were preparing for a fair. He'd cleaned its large red carpet the day before, and we'd stretched it out on the driveway to dry. Mark started to vacuum it, and ten minutes later, he called me.

"Look," he said, pointing at the rug. "Those are ashes falling on it."

Maybe the ashes should have warned us, but we couldn't see any flames. There was no smoke, no noise. Only soft white powder kept landing on the carpet.

"I give up," said Mark. He turned off the vacuum cleaner. The only sound now was the wind. "It sure is windy," I said. I went back inside and turned on the television. News reporters had started talking about a fire in Altadena, and they showed pictures of fire engines lined up on streets about a mile west of us. They weren't doing anything, just waiting. It was quiet outside.

At about seven o'clock, Mark walked down to the end of our street. As soon as he left, I heard a new sound. It was more than wind. It was a roar, not loud, but huge somehow. Then I felt the heat.

Just then Mark ran back. "Get in your car and get out of here," he shouted. "All of Kinneloa Villa is burning!" Kinneloa Villa was a community of big houses west of ours. "I just saw a policeman drag a woman in a nightgown out of her house!"

Just then Marvin ran out of the house and headed directly for my car. He screamed and scratched at the door. Smart dog, I thought. No sense in leaving on foot when you can have a ride. I let him into the front seat and slammed the door.

I ran back into the house and assembled the items that were to become my only pre-fire mementos. I grabbed some equally useful items for Mark, too: his least-comfortable shoes and a mismatched outfit. He didn't get any underwear at all.

When I came outside, the eaves of the house across the street were blazing, and the house beyond it was burning too. The roar was loud now, the heat frightening. Mark screamed at me from the roof, where he was wielding a fire hose barefoot. I screamed back at him.

"Leave!" he yelled. "I'll be right behind you!"

Sixty foot flames were swirling down the hill above us. "You've got to come, too!" I yelled.

"I will!" he screamed. "Just get going!"

And so I left. As I did, I realized what had seemed so odd. There was no sound except the roar of the fire itself. No sirens, no helicopters. Just that quiet roar and the heat. Two blocks away, life was normal. Bathrobed ladies were just stepping outside to pick up their papers. How could they know that fifty houses were burning less than a mile away? There was no smoke, no sound, and we weren't on television. It was just a crystal clear autumn morning, and time for a cup of coffee.

You Can't Go Home Again

I headed for Mark's parents' house on Riviera Drive. Over-looking Hastings Canyon, it was square in the path of the fire. I'll tell you now that it didn't burn. Firefighters arrived in droves, and the sound of helicopters laboring up the mountainside went on all day. They couldn't contain the fire, and they couldn't direct it, but by soaking hillsides and roofs, they were able to save dozens of houses.

It was a slow motion day, a surreal blur. I was mesmerized by the fire as it swept over the mountains in front of me. I watched a whole ridge line erupt in a series of explosions as the flames reached houses, cars and gas lines. Before the sun went down, the flames had blackened every slope I could see.

That night Mark and I lay on a bed in our clothes. Through the window, we could see flames still burning on the mountain. We slept fitfully, and before dawn, we got up. "Let's go home," said Mark. We made a thermos of coffee and climbed into his car.

At the bottom of our hill, a policeman was manning a barricade. He was surrounded by gawkers, but no one was getting through. "If you're a resident, you can go up in a police vehicle," he explained. "But you have to have identification."

Identification. I had mine in my purse, but Mark had left home the day before in shorts and a T-shirt. He'd had no time to go inside.

The officer looked at my driver's license, and then turned to Mark. Was it the sooty shirt, the wild hair? Without a word, he moved the barricade aside and said, "A van will be here in a few minutes to take you up."

The van turned out to be a paddy wagon, and we climbed into the cage in the back. Another man we didn't know joined us, and we began the ascent.

Everything looked serene and normal for the first half mile. Dawn was breaking on another cloudless day. Then we saw the first gap, a big black hole where a house was supposed to be. Then another, and another. By the time we reached the top of the hill, we'd counted at least a dozen.

I'd known all day yesterday that our house had burned, but we'd had no actual proof. Now, as we neared the last corner, I wondered. Could it somehow have survived?

The van turned the corner, and we saw our block. The two houses that were burning when I left were still standing. Ours was gone. The driver opened the door and said, "I'll be back later." Mark and I stepped outside. The ground was still hot.

"Look, there's the shower stall," I said. Black and leaning, it was the tallest thing.

Near the road stood two old chairs we'd set out for the Salvation Army to collect. "Well, that's handy, anyway," said Mark, and we sat down. It was time for a cup of coffee.

Archaeologists in Tarzan's Garden

How many glorious places have gone up in smoke? Athens, Rome, Chicago. As we sat on our cast-off lawn chairs surveying the smoldering wreckage, I thought of Aeneas fleeing burning Troy, carrying his grandfather and his household gods.

No, I didn't. I can think of that now, but then, I just sat there. We weren't looking at the ashes of Priam's palace. Our smoking citadel was only a shower stall. It wasn't noble, glorious, or even tragic, just a shock.

Even so, the archaeologist in me awoke immediately. "Look at the cars!" I said to Mark. We'd each left in a car, but there had been nothing we could do about two other vehicles parked in our driveway. One belonged to a man who worked for Mark's property management company, and the other to a friend who'd moved to New York. They had been parked right next to each other.

The Volkswagen Rabbit was incinerated. The engine block had liquefied and poured out of the engine compartment, creating a decorative aluminum bas relief on the asphalt. The body was blackened, the windows were gone, and the inside was devoid of anything except a couple of seat springs and a skeletal steering wheel.

Right next to it, the Chevette looked fine at first glance. Actually, two tires were melted and the paint had bubbled on one door, but two days later, Manny drove it away. "How could the fire be so selective?" I asked. "They were practically touching."

We spent the morning poking into the rubble and marveling. Most things were utterly gone, but we found a few interesting artifacts. The heat of the fire had delaminated a quarter and puffed it up like a little metal balloon. A can of pennies was now a solid cylinder of copper.

We stood where we guessed our china cabinet had been, the one from which I'd extracted the arrowhead on my way out. Fifteen feet long and eight feet tall, it had been made out thick slabs of Honduran mahogany by a friend whose cabinets were works of art. It must have burned like a dream. The concrete upon which it had stood was completely bare.

"I thought we'd find globs of silver or something," said Mark, "Melted, like the car engine." But there was nothing. My grandmother's tea service was somewhere over Santa Monica in a big black cloud.

We continued our exploration, careful to sidestep smoldering coals. We'd both melted holes in our sneakers by now, and the sun was climbing. It was shaping up into another hot, windy day.

"Okay, here's the storeroom," said Mark. The piles of rubble and ash were a little deeper. We'd both picked up sticks, and I poked into a steaming pile. It was a large rectangle of what looked like bedsprings. "We didn't have a bed in here," I said. "What was this?" Mark picked his way over and had a look. "It's the Slinkies," he said.

The storeroom had housed the inventory of a new retail business Mark and I had started a few months before. Wizards of Wonder, WOW for short, sold puzzles, games, and unusual toys at music festivals and county fairs. Our holiday inventory had begun to arrive, and most of it hadn't been unpacked. We'd ordered cases and cases of Slinkies, a perennially popular Christmas present.

We picked our way over the rest of the cement slab that formed the footprint of our erstwhile home. My computer had vanished entirely. The only high-tech remnants were the little metal sliders from three floppy disks. Near where my desk had been a filing cabinet was still recognizable. It had cooled enough for Mark to touch, and he pried it open with a crowbar he'd brought along in his back pack. "You never know," he said. "And it sure would be nice to have our tax records." It was empty.

Our house was unique. Built nearly a century before by Abbott Kinney, one of Los Angeles' early land barons, it had served as the livery stable for the Big House. The Big House burned down in the thirties, and nobody knew any more exactly where it had been. The stable building and the stone pump house on the edge of the reservoir were the last remaining structures of Kinney's estate. The hillside was studded with oaks, palms and eucalypti, and a stream carried water from a spring farther up the mountain to the reservoir, which was home to several hundred blue gill, catfish and bright orange carp. Legend held that there were bass in there, too, but we never spied one.

Mark had created a home inside the redwood shell of the old barn, and turned the pump house into a cozy den overlooking the reservoir. He'd never thought his hillside retreat was big enough for two, but he found space for me when we got married in 1990. He'd lived there for three years when I joined him, but he hadn't been alone. He shared his jungle with a cat, three ducks, a pack of coyotes, a family of skunks, a raccoon commune, and an occasional mountain lion. Peacocks and a blue heron visited the reservoir, which had grown to look like a natural lagoon. Wild mint and raspberries grew along the stream. It was hard to believe that Tarzan's dream house existed in the hills above Pasadena. Few people had any inkling it was up there, only half an hour from downtown Los Angeles.

We looked down the denuded hill past the black trunk of a headless palm tree to the old pump house. Built of native stones, it had a brick chimney and a shake roof. A perforated pipe ran along the ridge, and we'd left the water running the day before in the hopes that the roof might survive the fire if it were wet enough.

The pipe was still there, bent and black, but intact. Little puffs of steam burst from the holes. The roof was gone, and we could see red clay floor tiles through the rubble on the floor. We climbed down carefully and stepped inside.

Our eyes fell first on the iron harp of my grandmother's upright piano. It had smashed tiles when it hit the floor. Then we caught sight of something else. A ceramic vase was standing upright on a broken tile. Chartreuse and hideous, it was also intact and pristine. It looked like someone had just set it there.

"That vase," I said. "Do you remember how we got it?" Mark couldn't remember. "It was one of the gifts at the white elephant party we had last year. It was so ugly no one would take it home. I stuck it into one of the cabinets against the far wall. It was on the top shelf. How the heck did it get down here without breaking?"

"I think," said Mark, "That even forest fires have their standards. It took one look at that thing and said, 'No thanks. Even I don't want that.'"

When we arrived back at the top of our smoldering acropolis, we stood near our former kitchen sink, now a dented cast iron relic lying on its side on the ground. A eucalyptus tree nearby burst into fresh flames, and we looked down over the blackened lagoon.

I said, "You know, Mark, this is, in fact, amazing."

Mark says I said, "You know, Mark, this is, in fact, great."

However I started out, I continued, "We're cleaned out. There's nothing here, nothing at all. We can do anything we want. Anything. Do you know what that means? We can go anywhere, do anything, start over again. Whatever. I think we should think of this as an opportunity. I think it just could be the most amazing thing that's ever happened to us. I think..."

"Shut up," said Mark. "Shut up and give me five minutes to grieve."

View From The Black Gap

I shut up. He was right. I was chattering. I stood at the edge of the concrete slab and looked out over the San Gabriel Valley. I could see all the way to the ocean, which was a big change from the last time I'd stood in that place and looked south. Thirty trees had met their end, but the view they left behind was terrific.

I stood there and knew I was right. This really was amazing, maybe even great. All my stuff was gone, and that meant I had a clean slate. Yes, it meant that irreplaceable mementos were gone forever, but so were forty years of sediment, a serious buildup of tartar and plaque. Yes, my great grandmother's wedding dress was vapor, but so were thirty boxes I'd dreaded having to sort. For every item I mourned, there was a corresponding bushel of ballast that had held me hostage.

I felt the lightness immediately. I was a hot air balloon, and my tethers had just been cut. I gave Mark a full half hour to grieve.

"Let's hit the road," I said as we waited for the paddy wagon to come and get us. "The timing couldn't be better. We've got no stuff, no business, and no house to worry about. Let's just start driving and see what we find."

Mark didn't say yes, and he didn't say no. We rode down the hill and drove back to his parents' house. By this time, people were everywhere, surveying the wreckage. The policeman at the barricade was fending off a crowd of looters carrying shopping bags.

Meanwhile the fire was still burning its way eastward unabated. The winds were still high. My parents' house in the village of Sierra Madre was in its path. Blocked roads meant we couldn't go there, but we spent the day watching television and the weather. By midnight, the Sierra Madre Volunteer Fire Department and the winds pushed the fire north into the wilderness, and the town was left untouched. The next day, the air was still.

The fire did not leave a peaceful wake. Within hours, platoons of insurance agents arrived. Almost as fast came the contractors, carpet cleaners, "salvage experts" and "private adjusters," vultures attracted by a fresh disaster. On hundreds of scorched lots, men with tape measures and blueprints and clipboards brought bag lunches and folding chairs and stayed all day.

I escaped for the weekend to a meeting I'd planned to attend months before. I had no house, but I did have a hotel reservation. I stopped at a shopping mall on the way and bought some underwear and a shirt and a pair of jeans.

When I got back to Pasadena, Mark had joined a crew of volunteers who were preparing to sandbag the hillsides. Fire in Southern California mountains practically guarantees mud slides as soon as it rains, and they can be just as devastating as fire.

We went out to dinner Sunday night. While we waited for the waiter to take our order, Mark said, "Let's hit the road. Let's just start driving and see where we end up." I have no idea what we ate that night, but we stayed a long time. The waiter filled our coffee cups four times.

Fire. What a thing. Houses, trees, stuff, all gone in a flash. I'd been looking at the black gaps, but now, suddenly, I was looking at the view they'd left behind. I was a balloon, slowly rising over a fresh new landscape. The journey had begun.

The Stuff of Life

If life in the last decade of the century in America is a solar system, stuff is its sun. Our lives revolve around it, and its absence creates a powerful vacuum, the kind nature abhors. If you don't believe it, try this simple experiment. Divest yourself of all your stuff, and remain stuffless for a month. Okay, I'll allow you one suitcase, but that's it. See if you can avoid busting out of it for four short weeks.

Maybe the simplest road to unencumbered success would be to buy a Eurail pass and relive the days when you traveled light and traded paperbacks in youth hostels. Maybe you can find yourself a monastery and embark on a month-long retreat in a cell without closets. One thing's certain, though. If you stay where you are and follow the stuff-attracting patterns that define American life, your suitcase won't just bulge at the end of a week. It'll explode. By the end of the month, you'll be the curator of a brand new archive. Inexorably following its law, your stuff will have expanded to fill all available space.

Back in the seventies, when the Shah of Iran was sent into exile, hundreds of American expatriates left with him. A friend of mine was a teacher in Tehran at the time. One day while he was at school, he received instructions to drive to the airport, leave the keys in his car's ignition, and get on a plane. He left a large, nicely furnished apartment full of mementos of a life of travel and an Ivy League education. When I met him in Germany a few years later, it was in the living room of his large, nicely furnished apartment. Conspicuously devoid of Persian rugs, it nonetheless displayed ample evidence of a love of travel, a fascinating life. "Sometimes you have to swap possessions for experience," he said.

After a disaster, a giant machine mobilizes, and its motto is, "Put Everything Back." Government agencies like FEMA and the SBA arrive in a blizzard of forms in triplicate. Insurance adjusters explain about "replacement value," and "policy limits." Vaporized homes are recreated on paper, and the stuff they contained fills sheet after sheet of foolscap. Everywhere, scores of people began work immediately to do what people do after catastrophes: make everything look the way it did before.

But what if you were thinking, "Well, thanks, but I'm not so sure I want everything back just the way it was. After all, how many times do you get to start over in life? Isn't this a good time to stop and think a while? Isn't it a chance to maybe do something different?"

A perfect place to think materialized magically for Mark and Marvin and me. It was a guest house on a secluded estate in the town of San Gabriel. Designed as the ultimate entertainment pad, it had a huge living room, three bathrooms, and one bedroom. Sliding glass doors opened on one side to a camellia garden, and on the other to a large swimming pool. It was beautiful, which made us smile. It had enormous closets, which made us laugh.

Don't get me wrong. I love stuff. I love the people who brought us stuff when we had none. Family, friends, and strangers gave us clothes, furniture, dishes, pots, books, a bed, a table, food, a computer, and money. We were, quite literally, showered with gifts. Without them, life would have looked awfully bleak. After all, we live in three dimensions, where down comforters feel good on a chilly night, a dining room table is a great convenience, and china plates lend elegance to the simplest meal. I have never appreciated ordinary household stuff more than I did while I lived at the secret villa. It had appeared out of thin air. It was magic. It was love.

Christmas Came Anyway

We lived at "The Villa" for five months, from November, 1993, until March, 1994. One day in December, a package tied with string arrived, forwarded by the post office from our former address. It had German stamps and an illegible customs declaration stuck to the top. At first, I was baffled, but then I remembered.

In 1990, Mark and I had taken a trip to Europe. From Athens, we'd taken a ship through the Corinth Canal north through the Adriatic to Venice. We rented a car and drove through the Alps to Bavaria. In Oberammergau, we stayed with friends who introduced us to one of the master wood carvers for which the town is famous.

Before we left, we commissioned a Christmas creche. Each December, we'd be receiving a piece or two until we had a complete cast of characters. The first Christmas, we got the Mary, Joseph, and baby Jesus. By the time everything went up in smoke, we'd added two shepherds, a goat, a cow, a donkey, and a couple of angels.

When Mark got home, I showed him the box. "Do you know what this is?" I asked. He, too, was puzzled for a minute, but then he smiled. "It's got to be the wise men," he said. We opened the package, pulled away the excelsior, and there they were, each holding his perfectly carved little gift, each looking intently in the direction of a recipient who wasn't there.

"Sorry, no baby Jesus here," I said as I set them on the dining room table. "I'm afraid you guys came to the wrong stable."

But they didn't, really. They proved that no matter what happens, Christmas comes. Christmas doesn't even require a baby Jesus. It comes anyway, and the wise men proved it that year by insisting on arriving at an empty rental cottage.

And Christmas did come. By the time it arrived, we'd celebrated my parents' fiftieth wedding anniversary and my birthday, and we'd announced our grand plan. We'd hung a huge map of North America on the living room wall, and we'd begun sticking pins in all the places we'd always dreamed of visiting.

The wise men stayed on our table through January. Before I packed them away, I wrote to the wood carver to explain what had happened and ask him to start over. "We need a new holy family," I wrote, "And shepherds and animals and angels. Everything but the wise men."

Next Christmas, even if we had no table to set them on, the wise men would have something to look at, a reason for bearing gifts. I figured it was the least I could do for them, since they'd traveled 6,000 miles on faith, and arrived just when we needed some.

And now, we were about to follow our own star, with not much more than faith to fund it. We were fairy tale youngest sons, the ones who pack a bandana and leave home on foot to seek their fortunes. Maybe we should have followed their lead, but we were post-Ford children, and we needed something more. Before we could hit the road, we had to find ourselves a vehicle.

· 2 ·

A Phoenix Hatches

Trek to Traveland

Before we decided we wanted to acquire one of our own, neither Mark nor I had done much more than peek inside a motorhome. As children, we'd camped in tents with our families. We'd felt superior to people who didn't like "roughing it," overly civilized softies who couldn't be away from television for a weekend and felt compelled to tow their own bathrooms. Never in a million years did we see ourselves as members of the Winnebago crowd.

We still didn't, but we also didn't want to hit the road in a tent. If we were going to live on a roll for six months, we wanted a few amenities. Suddenly, we had metamorphosed into the people we'd snickered at. We'd be equipped with television. We'd be hauling our own toilet.

It was a novel idea for us, but Americans have been in love with recreational vehicles since 1929, when the Covered Wagon Company in Mt. Clemens, Michigan, offered the first mass produced travel trailer to the public. By the end of the 1930's, 300 companies were building homes-on-wheels, and the growth continues. Hundreds of thousands of vans, trailers, campers and motorhomes are on the road at any given moment today, and even more fill storage yards and driveways from coast to coast. We wanted only one, but we were daunted at the prospect of finding it. We hardly knew where to begin.

Fortunately, just about every motorhome, camper, and trailer ever built can be found and purchased in southern California. It's an RV shopper's Mecca, rivaled only by Florida and Arizona. We decided to begin our search at a gigantic consortium of dealers known as Traveland USA. Its billboard promised hundreds of manufacturers and thousands of units, all in one magnificent location. It was the kind of place we'd heretofore assiduously avoided, but early one Sunday morning, we drove straight to Irvine and parked in the shadow of fourteen Winnebagos.

A guard at an entrance kiosk gave us a map to Traveland that identified all the manufacturers and their locations. Not knowing where else to begin, we went to number one. It was a warm day, and a salesman was lounging in a folding chair outside an office in a trailer. He stretched, rose, and walked toward us.

"Howdy, folks," he said. "How can I help you this fine, fine morning?"

"We want to buy an RV," said Mark. "What can you show us?"

The salesman looked at us through narrow eyes, sizing up the down payment we were likely to represent. He steered us in the direction of something called a Jamboree, a boxy-looking vehicle about the length of two sedans. It was white, with corrugated siding and a front end like a pickup truck. We climbed inside, and the salesman invited us to sit down on the settee.

Realizing immediately that we were ignorant "first-time buyers," the salesman launched into a well-rehearsed 30-minute lecture about recreational vehicles. By the time he wrapped up, we'd learned the difference between a Class "A" (a bus) and a Class "C" (the kind we were sitting in). We knew about GVW (gross vehicle weight) and how important it was to know how much stuff you can load into a vehicle before the axles break. We knew about water tanks and propane tanks, generators and refrigerators, wind shear and suspension, inverters and converters, water pumps and fuel pumps.

While he was talking, I was taking in my surroundings. It was pretty spacious, I thought. I could live in this. There was a bedroom in the back, and another bed over the cab. The galley looked adequate, and the dining table seated four. What more did we need?

Suddenly Mark asked, "Does anybody make an RV with four-wheel drive?"

The salesman shrugged. "Well, actually there is one company that does. It's expensive, and it has no resale value, so I can't imagine anybody buying it, but there's one sitting on the lot here somewhere."

That did it. We thanked the salesman and said we'd be back if the Jamboree turned out to be the right truck for us. "Whatever you decide, I'd sure like to have a shot at the deal," he said forlornly as we departed. He sat back down in the folding chair, and we set off to find the four-by-four.

We asked the guard. "Oh, that thing," he said. "It's about a hundred yards around that bend to the right. You'll recognize it when you see it." We walked down the road and looked at all the vehicles with new eyes. "Class 'A'," I said, pointing to a huge bus with a patriotic mural on the side and an enormous satellite dish on the roof. "I can't see us driving around in anything that conspicuous."

"Well, I can't see us driving around in a Jamboree," said Mark. "It looked nice, but it had a flimsy feel. Did you noticed how far it leaned when we stepped inside? It's basically made of plywood and fiberglass. Doesn't anybody build these things like aircraft?"

We rounded the bend and stopped dead in our tracks. "That's it," said Mark, "Look at that thing." I looked. It was huge. It had six enormous tires and a big winch on the front bumper. The body was smooth and streamlined, and five driving lamps each had covers that read "Super Off-Roader." Mark smiled, and we headed toward the office to find somebody to let us inside.

You Say You Want A Revolution

But here I must digress. I've got to issue a warning to all those who say they want a revolution. This was November 10, 1993. The preceding December, I'd turned forty. It hit me like Dorothy's house hit the witch.

I was morose for days. I went about my daily drill, but I was a rusty tin man, forcing unwilling joints to move in directions they resisted. Life was toil. It wasn't unbearable, though, and I kept at it. I kept putting on nylons and checking my voice mail.

I told myself I wanted a revolution. I said it silently, but it shrieked in my head. It kept yelling for ten months. For ten months, I kept putting on nylons and checking my voice mail.

Then my house burned down. I got my revolution.

I didn't have to accept its offer of transformation. I could have put everything back, down to last pair of panty hose. It would have been easier. It would have made lots of people more comfortable.

But how many revolutions do you get in life? I hadn't had enough to waste one. However it might turn out, I'd turned enough degrees to have a whole new view in front of me.

It seemed monumental, but the fire, it turns out, was just a little baby vortex, a personal whirl that invited me to a new life. I didn't know as I stepped inside a Super Offroader at Traveland that I was on the edge of a Charybdis of global dimensions.

You were, too. We all were. 1994 was the year we heard "Information Superhighway" until we were sick of it. It was the year we got to know Bill Gates, and began tossing "Internet" into casual conversation.

America hit the road to cyberspace in 1994, beginning a revolution we've only begun to understand. It envelopes the world, and we can't ignore it. If we keep putting on nylons and checking voice mail, we'll be left in the dust.

The five years we've spent letting America's highways unroll underneath our wheels are the same five years Americans have moved into virtual realms. We've watched it happen in Eastern Oregon, northern Idaho, southern Texas, the Florida keys. No one's driven a golden spike, but it's no less monumental than the completion of the transcontinental railroad.

But enough. Please join us as we step inside the Super Offroader. Take a look at the ultra-macho truck we decided to call home for the six months that never ended. It's about to embark on a journey you've been on, too.

The Trailblazer

We caught the saleswoman just as she was about to leave. She got back out of her car, unlocked her office, and took the key to the Super Off-Roader off a hook on a peg board. We walked back out to the monster, and she unlocked the coach door.

As the door opened, two steps magically slid out from under the body and clicked into place. To anyone who knows anything about motorhomes, this would come as small surprise. To us, it was one more new thing, and I have to say, it made the Super Off-Roader seem terrifically cutting edge. We stepped up and inside.

"Take your time looking around," called the saleswoman from outside. "I'm going back to the office to get a video to show you. I'll be right back." The door clicked shut with satisfying heft. "This is more like it," said Mark.

To the right of the door was a bleached oak panel of electronic entertainment devices, including a television, a CD changer and a video player. A table flanked by two benches faced us, and to our left was the galley. Over the cab was a bunk that looked big enough for two. The cab itself held four captain's chairs.

A hallway led to the back room, which housed a table and a wrap-around sofa against three walls. All in all, the Super Off-Roader looked like a cross between a mobile military command post and a party wagon. It was the ultimate in manliness, the sort of rig guys dream about taking their buddies hunting in, no women allowed.

I sat down at the table, trying the thing on for style. It felt like a status symbol. It felt like a machine designed for the same men who buy red convertibles and marry trophy wives. It was a quantum leap beyond the bus-like monster with the satellite dish and the patriotic mural. "This thing defines conspicuous consumption," I thought to myself, "And it positively screams Southern California."

It was also built like an aircraft. The carpeted walls sloped in at the top, and the cabinets were cut to fit. Nothing was corrugated. Nothing was fiberboard. "Sleek" says it the best.

The saleswoman returned with the video. She slid it into the video player and said, "Now you can see the Trailblazer in action." The Trailblazer. Now we knew its name, and for the next ten minutes we watched two men take a similar machine over boulders and across streams to music that sounded like a cross between "Rawhide" and "Chariots of Fire."

When it was over, Mark asked the saleswoman a bunch of questions, but I knew we weren't going to be doing any more shopping. 99.99% of motor homes built in America are designed with 60-ish couples in mind. They're suburban split-levels squeezed and shrunk to fit inside a rectangle eight feet wide and 30 feet long. They've got upholstered window treatments, matching throw pillows, and built-in spice racks.

The Trailblazer was more like a ski hut reduced to fit on a one-ton Ford truck chassis, which of course didn't match our profile, either. But Corey, the saleswoman, had divulged another piece of information in passing. "You can follow your Trailblazer from chassis to completion," she'd said. "We can customize the interior for you."

"You mean we can have an office in the back?" asked Mark, "Instead of a party room?"

"I can't see why not," said Corey, "But you might want to visit our factory and talk to the designers."

We set a time to meet at the Revcon factory in Irvine, and stepped back outside the Trailblazer.

"It's huge," I said.

"I guess we need to know how much it costs," said Mark.

"$75,000," said Corey.

We thanked her and walked back toward the gate. $75,000 was three times more than we'd thought about spending. The guy with the Jamboree had been right on target when he'd sized us up.

"We'll go see the factory, and then we can decide," said Mark, but it was too late. We both knew it. We'd finished shopping, even though we'd hardly begun. We'd picked our wheels, and now we had a new challenge: figuring out how to pay for them when our income was about to drop by 90%.

Lunch With The Suits

Money. We're all brought up to plan our lives around how much we have, how much we expect to have, and how afraid we are of not having enough. I'd always lived well within my means. I had a couple of credit cards, but I always paid them off every month. I'd used them as an easy way of buying stuff, a way to avoid writing checks or carrying cash. The only big debt I'd ever incurred was a house loan.

The fire burned up my good habits along with my stuff. When I saw how easily the things I'd always considered permanent metamorphosed into smoke and ash, it shook all my assumptions. I'd always known anything could happen, but now I'd experienced it. There's a difference.

Two days after the fire, I put on my one remaining business outfit, the one that had escaped destruction by being at the dry cleaners. I went to work, accomplished nothing, and then decided to have lunch at the University Club.

The University Club is a former old boys' bastion I had joined a couple of years before. It was a good place for quiet lunches with business associates, and a growing number of female members was lightening its heavily masculine atmosphere. Even so, when I walked in the door, the round members' table in the center of the room was occupied by a phalanx of men. Every one of them had twenty years on me.

The week before, I would have looked for another table. I would have eaten alone rather than sit surrounded by suits. They'd always intimidated me. Today, as I stood in the doorway, I found myself looking at them and asking, "What have I got to lose?" It almost made me laugh out loud when I realized I'd never been so entitled to answer, "Nothing!" I walked right over to the table full of men and sat down. They looked surprised, but they all murmured hello.

They went back to talking about the fire, which was the only topic of conversation all over Pasadena. None of them had been affected, and they were wondering what was going on up in the hills. "It's still burning," I said. "My house went two days ago."

The conversation stopped. The whole table looked at me blankly. I was their first concrete example of burnout, and it silenced them. "It was all gone in a couple of hours," I said. "Just about the only things that survived were the cars we left in."

They didn't know what to say. They were all busy imagining what they'd be doing if their houses had burned down less than 48 hours before. They were having a tough time.

"I came here for lunch," I said, "Because I couldn't go home." I laughed, and they stared at me again. That's when it hit me. They were scared. They thought that losing all their stuff was the worst thing that could happen to them. They'd spent a lifetime piling it up and guarding it. They couldn't imagine what it was like to have it all snatched away, just like that, poof!

And then another thought struck me. They were supposed to be the powerful ones, the ones who intimidated the likes of me. But now they looked like slaves to the pursuit of security. I felt free. I smiled sweetly at them as they remained speechless. I think I spoiled their lunch.

Somehow, the fire had singed my soul. It ignited a thousand cliches with new meaning. If not now, when? Life's not a dress rehearsal. Be here, now. Follow your dreams. Climb every mountain. What are you waiting for? What have you got to lose? Just do it!

They were all shouting at me as we drove away from Traveland wondering how in the world we could buy a $75,000 truck. "Just do it!" drowned all rational doubts, and the next morning, we drove to Irvine to take a look at the Revcon factory.

Bastard Hunting

Revcon was housed in an industrial park, one of the thousands that have taken root in Orange County where citrus groves used to thrive. Anonymous on the exterior, they can surprise you with wonders on the inside. I once went into one that was a sculptor's studio, and another that was full of trombones, tubas, and a fascinating fellow who repaired them. Outside, they're urban sprawl. Inside, they're secret entrepreneurial kingdoms.

Revcon's operation qualified as an industrial park wonder. Inside a large garage-like space were parked three Trailblazers in various states of completion. While our eyes were adjusting to the light, a walrus of a man lumbered over to greet us. Trotting along next to him was a little terrier of a sidekick.

"Welcome to Revcon," said the big one. "I'm Bob." We introduced ourselves. "And this is Wes," he said, elbowing his companion. "Wes does a lot of our design work." Wes smiled nervously, and we followed both of them inside the factory.

It smelled like glue, and the rat-tat-tat of power hammers and staple guns echoed. "I'll show you the assembly line first," said Bob. He had Mark by the elbow. Wes flanked him. I walked behind. He steered Mark toward the chassis of a one-ton Ford pick-up truck. "This is what we start with," he said. "And actually, we have to buy the whole truck and strip it down. Ford won't sell us just the chassis. Anyway, we stretch the frame, and then we build the coach."

We walked by the three Trailblazers that had progressed to the point of having bodies, and we went inside the last one. Two workmen were installing light fixtures. Bob was still talking, and Wes was still laughing nervously, but I'd stopped listening. I was moving in, if only mentally.

Then I heard Bob say, "They use them to hunt bastards," and I was again all ears. "Yeah, Saudi Arabian princes buy these things and take them out into the desert to pursue their favorite pastime, bastard hunting." He was loving our stunned looks, and he paused dramatically. "Bastards are these big birds they like to shoot." Oh. Bustards. I didn't bother telling him he had his vowel wrong. Without his malapropism, Bob would have been no fun at all.

By the time Bob escorted Mark into the front office and allowed me to edge in, too, before closing the door, I had formed some opinions. The first was that for Bob, cornering a potential customer in his office was as unusual as catching a leprechaun in a rat trap. The second was that Revcon was more than it appeared to be. Beyond the factory floor was a warren of offices full of boxes, telephones, mismatched furniture, and a dozen or so aimless young men wearing ties. People were either moving in, moving out, or incredibly disorganized. It was a mystery, along with the fact that Bob's office appeared to belong to someone else, someone with a German name.

In any event, Trailblazers were definitely being built, and Bob was bursting to sell us one. The price was $75,000, just as Corey the saleswoman had said. There was no negotiation. That was the price. We could follow our truck from chassis to completion. In fact, the chassis we'd just seen would be ours. And yes, they'd work with us to create an office in the back in place of a bedroom, and they'd wire in any equipment we wanted, like a CB radio, a cellular telephone, whatever. So do you want it? Please sign here. By the time we were done, I felt as though Bob had been sitting on me for three hours.

In the end, we signed, because, as I've said before, our good sense had been burned up in the fire. We walked back out to the factory to look at our chassis, which was supposed to become Coach Number 115 within six weeks. We didn't know it then, but it was a lucky thing for us that it took more like twelve. The extra time came in handy for scraping together $75,000.

Beyond the Cutting Edge

Perhaps at this point I should explain why we were more interested in offices than bedrooms. Even though we had only a vague notion about exactly why we were hitting the road at all, one component of the fog was work.

I was a fledgling freelance writer and newspaper columnist. My first column had been published the week before the fire, and I was determined to sell my editor on the idea that I would still file the thing regularly, whether I was in Outer Boondocks, Alaska, Off The Map, Maine, or Times Square. Nobody would be able to tell I wasn't still firmly planted in Pasadena, California, including him. I swore to it, so he said he'd give it a try. It helped that he was already heavily into computers and electronic communication. It also helped that I had a good track record with deadlines. I hadn't even missed the one that arrived two days after the fire, and that accomplishment had left a lasting impression.

So it was really that column, for which I was paid the princely sum of $25 a week, that led to our acquiring a mobile office equipped with $15,000 worth of electronic gadgets. To appreciate just how cutting-edge we were, think back to before "AOL" was only a typo for "AWOL," like 1993.

It was a day when few could understand why anyone would want to access the Internet by cellular telephone. Heck, it was a day when few had more than a vague idea about what the Internet was. I was one. I read a bunch of stuff, and still couldn't quite understand about onramps and service providers. I'd think I was beginning to catch on, but then I'd run into a POP, SLIP, or a BMP, and get stuck.

But 1993 was the year America Online began paving the continent with "free" disks. Every man, woman and child in the country received these disks on a regular basis. Every magazine on every newsstand had AOL disks stuck between alternating pages. You could walk through cemeteries and find one carefully propped against each headstone. Bars used them for coasters, contractors used them for insulation, and everybody used them for doorstops. There were so many AOL free disks thrown into New York trash cans that the landfill at Freshkill was closed two years ahead of schedule. When AOL stopped sending them out, the U.S. Postal Service laid off two thousand workers. Okay, okay, I've overstated things a little. But it is true that I had three AOL disks before I owned a computer to try them on, and my friend's dog had two.

Fortunately, I knew a computer consultant who was fluent in both English and Nerd. We told him what we wanted to do, and he found all the stuff to do it. Then he taught us how to use it, all in perfect, uncondescending English.

Here's what we got, and in January, 1994, it was bleeding edge. The laptop was a Zenith Data Systems 486 with a color monitor and a 502-megabyte hard disk. It had a slot on one side into which you could stick a PCMCIA "credit card" modem. The one I got boasted a baud rate of 14,400 which was twice as fast as most people's regular modems at the time. I also got a separate box that could read CD-Rom disks, a SCSI cable to hook it to the computer, a Hewlett-Packard portable ink jet printer, and a black case to hold everything, including a snake nest of cables and assorted transformers, batteries and power packs.

So big deal. 1994 was the year thousands and thousands of people were diving into computerland with open checkbooks. Everything I had so far was new, but hardly unique.

Then we got the black box. It arrived with no instructions, but its manufacturers claimed it would make a cellular telephone talk to a modem. The black box was our key to mobility, but it was a silent enigma. Our computer consultant knew nothing about it. I called the customer service number on the box it arrived in. The person who answered the phone knew nothing about it. I'd arrived at the edge of charted territory, and I was on my own.

· 3 ·

The Epicenter of Burning Desire

Itching For Adventure

Itching is romantic when it means desire, and in the days Mark and I spent planning our grand journey, the word aptly described our yen for adventure. It was a pleasant itch, one we were eager to indulge. Little did we know, in those halcyon days when our travels were unsullied by genuine experience, that there would come a day when all notions of sentimental scratching would be routed by a real-life invasion of starving fleas.

Or maybe they were ticks. Whatever sort of bloodsucking pests they were, about a million of them hitched a ride when we pulled into a truck stop near Albuquerque, New Mexico. We'd taken Marvin for a walk before going to sleep. The parking lot had just been resurfaced with a layer of asphalt the consistency of blackstrap molasses. "Oh, great," I said as I peeled my shoe away from the ground at every step. "This will be with us forever." Marvin hadn't liked it much, either, and we'd headed for a dusty field full of sage brush where he could walk without sticking.

We retired for the night. In the morning, Mark woke up scratching. Pretty soon I was scratching, too. From the look of him, Marvin had been scratching all night.

A closer look revealed armies of minute black bugs marching across his belly, entrenched around the edge of each ear, and bivouacked between his toes. He was swarming with them from nose to tail. Suddenly I remembered that he'd slept in our bed most of the night. Not only that, he'd spent at least an hour on my head. It had rained during the night, and Marvin was frightened by the thunder. Excuse me while I scratch. Just writing this is making me itch all over again.

I am a person who believes that one tick is hideous beyond description. One is enough, when you think about what it does. It screws its head into your vein and bloats on your blood. More often than not, you don't notice it until it's a foot long. When you finally discover it, it's like realizing you've been hosting a body snatcher. You scream. If you're in the shower, it scares your husband. When he sees why you screamed, he screams, too.

This situation was so extreme it rendered us both speechless. Mark held Marvin down, and I set to work with a pair of tweezers. It was a Sisyphean task, like mowing a football field with nail clippers.

If you rolled bagels in them, you'd swear these things were poppy seeds. You wouldn't notice the difference until you took a bite. Then you'd make the delightful discovery that your mouth was full of little balloons bursting with blood. They popped when I pinched them. It was a gory scene.

I stayed at my task for an hour or so, and the war was still far from over. "I'll keep up the attack as we go," I said to Mark. "I hope you don't itch too much to drive."

I searched and destroyed all day, taking breaks only to scratch and wash blood and body parts off my hands. The bugs fought back by dropping to the floor and scurrying into corners. I added a Dust Buster to my arsenal and kept on fighting. By the time we arrived in Las Vegas, the enemy was in full retreat.

Money, Money, Money

Have you ever noticed how, once you have resolved on a course of action, life's minutiae mobilize to thwart your best-laid plans? Distractions attack from every quarter, just like an invasion of bloodsucking bugs. How can you concentrate when you itch? How can you progress when you're constantly pausing to scratch? Sometimes, in the months we spent getting ready to hit the road, I had the feeling we might never actually do it. We were too busy swatting mundane distractions.

And even now, psychic fleas are pestering me. Every time I set out to talk about money, I let them sidetrack me. Instead of facing my subject squarely, I find myself writing about mysterious black boxes or infestations of biting insects. But money, as it is wont to do, keeps floating back to the surface. This time, I swear, I won't pause to itch or scratch for at least a page.

There are two reasons money is a recurring theme. One is that people always ask us about it. The other is that we keep having to drum some up to stay on the road.

People usually ask an either-or question, something like, "Did you get a huge insurance settlement, or are you independently wealthy?" Having observed our itinerary and estimating how much gas a 7-ton monster guzzles, they figure those are the only two options. I would have thought the same a few years ago.

The fact of the matter is, there are other possibilities. They aren't the ones you'll read about in how-to-manage-your-money magazines. They only show up occasionally in interviews with people who have "beaten the odds": an illiterate man who manages to send eight children to college or a 45-year-old woman with cancer who climbs a peak in the Himalayas.

If the illiterate man had waited until he had enough money to educate his children, they would have grown up illiterate, too. If the woman with cancer had waited until she had enough money, well, forget it. Somehow, both completed projects that cost thousands and thousands of dollars they didn't have.

The fact of the matter is, money isn't what allows you to do things. It actually keeps you from doing things if you believe it has to come first. What really has to come first is resolve, a burning desire to accomplish something no matter what.

We did receive insurance money to cover the belongings inside our house. We used a large piece of it to pay business expenses: all the inventory we lost had not been paid for, and it was not insured. There was enough money left over to buy an inexpensive motorhome or make a down payment on a custom-designed one. The route we chose would make a financial advisor cringe.

It's been five years since we've received money on a regular basis or from traditional sources. We've used up our savings, we've worked, we've borrowed. On spectacular occasion, we've been visited by miracles. Sometimes we've felt hopelessly short of cash, and other times, we've felt as though we had plenty. We've been scared, and we've been confident, we've come close to giving up hope, and we've ridden high on waves of abundance. Every once in a while, as we're barreling down a highway on a fine day, we look at each other and say, "Well, here we still are." And we are. It must be magic.

If it is, then life is magic. Nobody waits for enough money to raise a child before they have one. They just go ahead and make things happen as the journey unfolds.

It wasn't money or its lack that sent us on the road. It was something far simpler. We wanted to. We wanted to more than we wanted to do anything else. We had a burning desire, appropriately ignited by a wildfire.

A Large Shake

By January, we were a few steps closer to rolling. The Revcon Trailblazer was slowly taking shape in the Irvine factory. It now had its own name, the Phoenix One. I'd wanted to call it Phoenix because it was rising from our ashes, and Mark said okay, as long as we added the One. "It means there might be a Two someday," he explained. "It's forward looking." We were forward looking, too. Most of our sentences began, "When we leave," or "Once we actually hit the road . . ." We were living in the future, and I was getting impatient for the future to be now.

Then, on January 17, 1994, something happened that riveted us to the present. It was still dark when the first jolt hit, and it threw me out of bed. By the time the second tremor rolled under us, I was wide awake, and Mark had joined me on the floor. Car alarms were screaming. Dogs were barking.

"Unless the epicenter is right where we are," I said, "This is a really big earthquake." Another series of shakes rattled our windows. I crawled over to the television and turned it on. Already, a disheveled announcer at a local station was on the air. Behind him, shelves had toppled. Books were scattered on the floor.

It was a serious quake, all right, 6.7 on the Richter Scale. The worst damage was sustained in the San Fernando Valley community of Northridge, where gas mains exploded, apartment buildings collapsed, and over 50 people died. Twenty-two thousand people were forced to leave their unsafe homes, and even more evacuated out of sheer fright. Public parks were transformed into tent villages, and the National Guard turned out to keep order. Once more, legions of insurance adjusters and FEMA staffers arrived in Los Angeles to set up temporary shop in the latest disaster zone. The fires of October were forgotten in the dust of crumbled freeways.

A friend of mine in North Hollywood lost the contents of his apartment. Everything was smashed, and he was in shock. I told Mark about it while we were eating dinner. "I wonder what we can do to help," I said. "Well," said Mark, "We've accumulated a lot of stuff that we aren't going to need when we hit the road. Maybe it's stuff he can use." It was true. What would we do with a microwave or china bowls? Only a crazy person would take crystal glasses on a road trip.

I called Rich the next morning, and the things we'd acquired matched remarkably well with what he had lost. We loaded up his car to the roof.

So I guess you could say that the earthquake cleaned us out, too, and we were happy it did. When we took to the road, we wanted nothing material tethering us to a specific spot, especially a storage locker. I'd travel to the edge of the world to see a friend, but an aging coffee maker is hardly a worthy grail.

While I'm still on the subject of earthquakes, I must share a bit of wisdom gained from experience. You've heard the standard admonishment, "When you feel a tremor, get in a doorway." I'd heard it, too, all my life, and I've even told other people. Well, folks, there's a little more to it than that. A friend of mine found out the hard way. When the Northridge earthquake hit, Barbara rushed to a doorway. As she stood there, another tremor struck. The doorframe hit her between the eyes. She lost consciousness briefly, and the next day, she had two black eyes. So remember, when an earthquake hits, go to a doorway, and CROUCH DOWN, COVER YOUR NECK AND HEAD, AND BRACE YOURSELF INSIDE THE FRAME.

The only other piece of useful earthquake advice I can share I heard from a Caltech seismologist. "If you live in Southern California," he said, "Push your expensive Scotch to the back of the shelf."

Wheels!

Slowly but surely, our Phoenix was rising. Mark drove to Irvine nearly every day to make sure it was rising to his satisfaction. I was still working at the job I'd held before the fire.

It got to be January. It got to be February. It got to be March. It got to be a week away from the day we were supposed to assume ownership of our new home.

We had started applying for loans the day we decided to have the Phoenix One built. We'd heard "no" three times. We were on the fourth application, and the prognosis looked no better. Why would a bank whose usual M.O. is to loan people only money equivalent to what they already possess, lend us a cent? We were crazies with an irresponsible gleam in our eyes. We were exactly the kind of loan applicants that lending agents are trained to escort firmly to the door.

With only a week to go, we needed a miracle. We needed a bank that would loan us $56,250 because they liked our smiles, one that would believe we meant it when we signed a piece of paper saying we'd pay it all back.

Eighteen hours before we were due in Irvine to assume possession of the Phoenix One, water turned into wine. The last bank, represented by a woman with a lovely smile, funded our loan. The next day, we drove to Irvine, signed a bunch of papers and kicked the tires one last time.

The Phoenix was ours! Mark climbed into the cab, turned on the engine, and pointed it toward Pasadena. I followed in the car. I tailed him along Irvine Boulevard as we headed for the freeway. Outside the rarefied atmosphere of the Revcon factory, the Phoenix stood out like Santa Claus in July. It stopped traffic. "My god," I thought, "We've bought an eyesore." A sharp pang of buyer's remorse struck me in the gullet. "I'm a conspicuous consumer. I'm a frivolous spendthrift. Those other three banks were right. We really are insane."

The Phoenix paused at a traffic light, then turned onto a freeway ramp. I followed. I had 26 miles to think about what we'd done. It only took two for me to recover from my momentary lapse. What did I care if the Phoenix drew attention? We'd picked it out because it was different. The ordinary possibilities hadn't appealed to us. They hadn't suited our new lease on life.

As we headed north, my mood rose like a hot air balloon. The truck rolling smoothly along the highway ahead of me meant everything we'd planned was suddenly real. We had our wheels! There was nothing stopping us! We were ready to roll! We were free!

We drove to Mark's parents' house. They came out. "It's beautiful," they said. My sister and brother-in-law came over to take a look. "It's obscene," they said. But everybody looked inside and outside. They climbed underneath and up on the roof. They sat at the table and lay on the bed and turned on the faucet and opened the cupboards. Before the afternoon was out, the Phoenix had attracted twenty gawkers, and it was parked on a secluded cul-de-sac.

I can't tell you who was right. Maybe the Phoenix was beautiful, and maybe it was obscene. I'd wondered myself whether it was good or bad, pleasing or offensive, right or wrong. But that night, as Mark and I lay down for the first time in our new bed, we fell asleep knowing that only one thing really mattered. The Phoenix was ours.

Four Cats In Santa Cruz

Wait a minute. Did I really say, "I was free" back there? I may have felt that lovely lighter-than-air ebullience as I drove back to Pasadena behind our new set of wheels, but it was fleeting. We'd just gained a car payment as big as a mortgage. Freedom? Maybe it really is a word for nothing left to lose. Maybe it's only a tantalizing abstraction to sing about on the Fourth of July, or to enjoy for a moment when all your worldly goods are gone, and you haven't had a chance to fill the vacuum.

The Phoenix filled a good chunk of the vacuum, and gradually, we were acquiring its contents. New stuff. Different stuff. Stuff I never knew existed.

Insurance companies are organized to make sure you replace all your old stuff with stuff that's as similar as possible.

If you had a couch, you pick out a new one. You work your way down your list, putting everything back. As long as you stick to the footprint of the stuff you lost, everyone is happy. Pretty soon, you can start forgetting that the fire ever happened. It fades like a bad dream at daybreak.

If, on the other hand, you decide that the fire wasn't so much a disaster as a chance to reinvent yourself, you're on your own. If you decide that in place of a couch, you would like a black box that will make a cellular telephone work with a modem, don't expect an insurance agent to understand. It won't make sense to anyone but you.

I didn't realize it at the time, but as I look back, most of our decisions about stuff revolved around keeping in touch. We could live happily without a dishwasher, but we couldn't leave town without a modem. We had no yen for a dining room table, but we couldn't depart without a computer, a printer, a telephone, and a fax machine.

Nearly half of the living space in the Phoenix One was dedicated to communication. The entire "back room," space which in most motor homes is filled with a bed and wardrobes, was an office, complete with desk, filing cabinet, slide-out shelf for the fax machine, and storage for computer equipment. One cabinet was reserved to hold all our clothes. Our bed was a bunk over the cab.

Now that the Phoenix really existed in three dimensions, our plans for departure began to solidify, but we still didn't know exactly when we'd actually climb into the cab and drive away. It's a funny thing when you plan to set forth on a journey of your own making. You can plan and plan and never quite get around to leaving. You need a deadline, or you can keep planning forever.

A deadline appeared at precisely the right moment. Mark's brother in Santa Cruz called. "We're going to Hawaii at the end of March," he said. "We need someone to house sit for us and feed the cats." Suddenly there was no more time for dreaming. The Phoenix One had a mission, a focus, a drop-dead date. Four hungry cats were counting on us to hit the road.

Meeting The Roadman

While we were in the midst of preparing for our departure, we received an invitation to attend an Indian meeting. The meeting was to be held at a friend's house in the mountains just north of the San Fernando Valley.

"It lasts all night," explained Catherine. "You should bring pillows, and Megan has to wear a dress. Also, bring food to share with the group."

An Indian meeting. My only knowledge of such things came from Carlos Castaneda, and lots of people said he made things up. "But why not?" said Mark. "It seems like a perfect way to start an adventure."

We arrived at the house around five-thirty and parked in front. A pick-up truck was parked in the driveway, and two men were sharpening a yucca stalk to a point in the front yard. A handful of other people were sitting on the porch. Catherine was in the kitchen. "Just bring whatever you brought on in," she said. "Things will be starting pretty soon."

Two men were moving furniture out of the living room. A serious man in a leather jacket seemed to be in charge. He said, "Let's build the altar now," and a thin teen-ager wearing combat boots and chains carried in four two-by-fours and dumped them on the floor.

"What are we supposed to do?" I whispered to Mark as seemingly random activity continued around us. Another man entered with a bag of sand over his shoulder. He dumped it on the floor. Another man arrived with a load of firewood. "I have no idea," said Mark. "I guess we just watch and see what happens."

The man in charge walked into the room. "What are all these pillows doing in here?" he demanded. "Get them out of here." He was pointing at our pillows, the ones Catherine had told us to bring. We stuffed them back into a corner, and shrank back on top of them.

A blonde woman in blue jeans arranged the four two-by-fours into a rectangle. The man who'd brought the sand arrived with another bagful and dumped it inside, right onto the floor. He added the other bag, and the rectangle was full. The woman used a flat stick to smooth and flatten the sand.

More people arrived carrying food. Catherine came to tell us that one of the women was the organizer of the meeting. "She's the one who called it," she said. "She's the one who will tell the Roadman why we're here."

The Roadman. The man in the leather jacket. I'll be very curious to find out why we're here, I thought. And why we're staying all night. It's going to be a long one.

What looked like chaos continued to swirl around us, but out of the seemingly random activity, an altar took shape in the middle of the room, a fire was laid in the fireplace, the women changed into dresses, and people arranged themselves in a circle, kneeling or sitting cross-legged on the floor. We were about thirty in all, a large group for a small living room. The roadman took his place directly across from us. The room was slowly filling with smoke.

The ritual unfolded before us, and much of it revolved around smoke and fire. The roadman had a beaded leather bag full of tobacco and cedar. He laid talismans on the altar. He filled a pipe, and we all smoked in turn. He talked to the woman who had called the meeting.

Our knees were already hurting, unaccustomed as we were to sitting immobile on the floor. We had at least twelve hours to go, maybe more.

"I'll pass the medicine," the Roadman was saying. "I want each of you to take four spoons." Catherine had told us about the medicine. "It's a peyote tea," she'd said. "And yes, it can make you sick. There are containers to throw up into, if you need them." Near us was a plastic gallon-sized milk jug with a hole cut in it, just big enough to hold a face. "It tastes horrible," Catherine had warned us. "In fact, I think it's the worst thing I've ever had in my mouth."

The bowl arrived. I downed my four spoons quickly, before I could change my mind. It's not so bad, I thought. It was bitter and herbal and odd, but down it went. I eyed the milk jug, but nothing happened. Piece of cake.

The room was smokier now, and darker. The only light came from the fireplace, where a young man with black, waist-length hair was tending the fire.

The ceremonies continued. There was chanting and praying and drumming. I saw demons in the embers. The Roadman across the room had a devil's face. A woman in a black dress had snakes in her hair. I watched and watched. I must have slept.

Three times during the night the Roadman passed the medicine. The rituals continued, the praying, the chanting. A bucket of water was passed around, and we drank in turn from a tin cup.

Dawn peeked in around the edges of the curtains, and the ceremony seemed to trail off. We found ourselves again surrounded by aimless activity. Some people lay on the floor. Others walked outside. The fire went out.

Somewhat dazed, we decided to put our belongings into our car. "Maybe we should just leave," whispered Mark. "Not a bad idea," I whispered back. It was already mid-morning, and there was no way of telling how long people might stay. A small group was chatting with the roadman at the other end of the living room. Catherine seemed to have disappeared. "No one will ever miss us," I added.

We picked up our pillows and walked outside. Before we reached the car, a voice called, "Wait!" We turned, and the Roadman was standing on the porch. He walked down the steps. "You aren't leaving, are you?" he asked. "You must come and eat."

How had he known we were leaving? He'd been ensconced in conversation twenty feet away when we slipped out. How had he crossed the room so fast? We went back inside the house.

Suddenly, we were part of the group. The Roadman, it turned out, was a Navajo from Phoenix. Other Native Americans had come even farther distances. Many participants were Caucasians who attended meetings of the Native American Church regularly. One woman had built a sweat lodge in her backyard. One man, a Hopi who lived in North Hollywood, had lost his apartment in the earthquake. "But I still have my truck," he said. "And my grandfather told me to come to this meeting." His grandfather had died three years before.

We feasted on the food everyone had brought, and finally the real time to leave arrived. Feeling much better than we had a few hours before, we climbed into our car and headed east, the opposite direction from which we had come.

Just why we drove off in the wrong direction is unclear to me now. Maybe it was difficult to turn around, and we thought we could "go around the block." Maybe it was the peyote. In any event, we found ourselves driving over the mountains in a dense fog. When visibility returned, we couldn't have been more surprised to find ourselves at Buttonwillow, a traveler's oasis on Interstate 5 about two hundred miles from any place we wanted to be. "We better not ever tell anybody about this," said Mark. We decided to rent a motel room and sleep.

Our rumps were still numb. The motel had a whirlpool, but even a half-hour soak failed to bring them back to life. They stayed numb for three days. By the time sensation returned, we'd begun to fear we'd never feel anything in our hind quarters again.

As we drove back to Pasadena the next morning, we agreed that the Indian meeting had been a transforming experience. "I have no idea in what way I was transformed," I said, "But something definitely happened."

"I still can't figure out how that Roadman knew we were leaving," said Mark. "Or how he got out onto the front porch so fast."

"I don't see how he did it, either," I agreed, "But then, I don't understand most of what happened there. Like how does a grandfather who's been dead for three years tell you to go on a road trip?"

But then again, maybe I do understand. It may be my imagination, it may be only a demon in a fireplace, but I swear there are times I hear my own grandfathers speak. I hear the voices of those who crossed the plains in wagons, and the older ones who crossed the Atlantic in sailing ships. It's not my own idea to hit the road. It's in my blood.

$\cdot 4 \cdot$

Already Gone

The Most Wonderful Road in the World

On March 27, 1994, a group made up of family and friends gathered in the backyard of Mark's parents' house. It was the same place where, four years earlier, we'd held our wedding reception, the same vantage point from which we'd watched the wildfire rage five months before.

We tied blue and white helium balloons from every available hook and handle on the Phoenix One's surface, and I wrapped a bottle of champagne in cheesecloth. With forty well-wishers standing by, I smashed it on the winch. Everyone cheered, and the Phoenix One was officially christened.

All afternoon, everyone inspected every corner of the Phoenix, flipping switches, flushing the toilet, turning on the television. Everyone wished us well, and some said they wished they were going with us. "There's one extra bed," we said. "Why not?"

When everyone left, Mark and I sat at the galley table. "I guess we're really going to do it," I said.

"Why is it so dark in here?" said Mark. He flipped a light switch. Nothing happened. "The batteries are dead," he said as he pushed the test switch. We had lot to learn about life on wheels, but that night, as we crawled into our cozy bunk, I'm sure the smile I fell asleep with lasted all night. The most wonderful nights in the world are the ones before long-awaited trips. The road lies ahead. Everything is possible. Anything can happen. The moment just before a dream comes true is the best moment of all.

Tuesday, March 29, 1994, was chilly and clear. We buckled Marvin into his new seatbelt harness, kissed our families goodbye, and climbed into the cab. We had to be in Santa Cruz by nightfall. Dan, his wife Lynette, and their three children had already left for Hawaii. The cats were waiting.

We drove west to join Interstate 5. The Phoenix struggled up Tejon Pass, and Mark, who'd had visions of roaring up the hill, was forced to join the line of eighteen-wheelers crawling along in the slow lane. "This won't do, this just won't do," I heard him grumble. It was fine with me, though. I was in no rush, and even the taste of diesel fumes couldn't dampen my mood. "We'll get there," I said, but I knew I wasn't talking to a rational being. I was talking to a man in a truck, and men in trucks brake at performance shops. I sighed. I was looking at a lot of hours in garages. We inched our way to the summit and descended into the San Joaquin Valley at Grapevine. Mark cheered up on the downhill slope.

Interstate 5 has been called the most boring highway in the world. It runs for miles through flat, dry fields, punctuated only by man-made installations of fast-food restaurants, motels and gas stations, each one competing for the tallest sign.

The first one we came to was none other than Buttonwillow, the same place we'd found ourselves when we got lost in the fog after the Indian meeting in the mountains. We'd left our new goose down pillows in a motel room there. We stopped at the office to see if we might retrieve them.

"Oh, yes," said the desk clerk. "I know exactly the ones. He disappeared and returned, holding the two pillows at arm's length. "Here you are," he said, suppressing a grimace. I took them, and immediately understood why. They reeked of stale smoke and incense.

"Maybe they'll air out," I said as we walked back to the Phoenix. "I don't know," said Mark. "Maybe we should drop them off at a toxic waste dump." But we stuffed them in the back. They finally lost their aroma, but even now, if I press my face deep into one, I can breathe in a faint reminder of our night with the Roadman.

We continued our run north, and the day was California perfect, which is another reason people think I-5 is boring. Oh, it might rain, and sometimes a dense fog will reduce visibility to zero, but you won't be met by a tornado, and the snow stays up on the mountains and passes. I-5 is straight, predictable, and fast, especially after the speed limit was raised to 65 miles an hour. Most people drive 70 or 80.

The flat road was perfect for finding out what the Phoenix could do when it wasn't trying to overcome a steep grade. Mark had driven it around Los Angeles, and we'd taken it on one overnight shakedown cruise to a beach near San Diego, but this was the first time we'd had the thing on a highway that stretched to the horizon. He floored it. "Vroom," said the Phoenix, and the speedometer needle jumped to the right. Mark smiled, and passed a big rig full of cows. I turned on the CD player. "I'm already gone," sang the Eagles. Suddenly, Interstate 5 was the most wonderful road in the world.

There are no words in the English language that speak to a man's soul louder than "4-wheel drive." The Phoenix had six wheels, four that drove and two that followed on a tag axle. Mark had yet to test his new 4-wheel power except in a parking lot. I wasn't surprised, as we headed north on the arrow-straight pavement, when he said, "Let's cut over to the coast on a road that offers some challenge. Look at the map. What are the possibilities?"

We were closing in on Kettleman City, another tiny town whose economy had been boosted by the arrival of a major highway. "Well," I said, we missed Highway 46, which is the usual way to cut over to Paso Robles and Highway 101, but there's this other road, Route 41. It's marked as a scenic road, and it passes Orchard Peak, which is 3,125 feet tall. Think that'll give you enough of a thrill?"

"I've never been on that road," said Mark, who had traveled many such byways during his tenure as a firefighter for the Forest Service. "Let's do it."

We made the turn onto a two-lane road that rose into low

hills. After three miles or so I caught sight of a sign. "RVs and Trailers Not Recommended," it read.

"We're an RV," I said.

"We have 4-wheel-drive," said Mark.

"But what if it's too twisty, or too narrow, or. . ."

"That sign was for Winnebagos and those huge house trailers. The Forest Service drives trucks up there, so we'll be fine."

I sighed. We were well past the sign now, anyway, and Mark was in the grip of 4-wheel fever. So far the road looked perfectly ordinary. Maybe the sign was for the overly cautious, or people who couldn't steer well.

We continued to climb, and, was it my imagination? The lanes seemed a little narrower. Mark took the Phoenix around a curve or two, and I looked over the drop-off on my side. This wasn't four-wheeling territory, but it was a road where you had to pay attention to turns. "Slow down," I said to myself, knowing that if I said it out loud, I'd be treated to a burst of acceleration.

The road got narrower. The turns got sharper. Mark had no choice but to slow down. "Maybe the sign was right," I thought, but it was too late to turn back, and it was pointless to verbalize the obvious.

We rounded a bend near what seemed to be the summit of the ridge we were climbing. Headed straight at us and half in our lane was a fire truck bearing the logo of the California Division of Forestry. Behind the wheel was a fireman with an open mouth. He screeched to a halt, and we inched around each other. He kept the baffled look the whole time.

It was the first time we'd surprised someone in isolated country, but it wouldn't be the last. We didn't know it then, but that baffled look would become a familiar sight. It meant, "Who are those guys? What is that truck? What are they doing out here?" If you drive a vehicle with NASA looks, you come to expect it.

Our back end hung out over a few more cliffs as we wound our way down to join Highway 46. The road had been a beginning lesson in the Phoenix One's strengths and limitations. Yes, it could climb hills and navigate corners, but no, it couldn't handle curves like a jeep. The wheel base was just too long, and no amount of four-wheeling can provide traction on a wheel that's spinning in mid-air.

Even though he never got to shift into 4-wheel-drive, Mark was happy with our little detour. I think he liked the look on the fireman's face. I was happy to be back on a flat road, with asphalt under all six wheels. We headed north on Highway 101, and cut over to the coast at Salinas.

Pizza At The Edge of the Continent

Is there a more idyllic city than Santa Cruz? Tucked between the mountains to the east and crashing waves to the west, its cool, moist air is the favorite atmosphere of coast redwood trees. There are always flowers blooming outdoors in Santa Cruz. It's a natural greenhouse for begonias, fuchsias, peonies — all those soft, hard-to-grow flowers the romantics immortalized in lavish still-life paintings.

Santa Cruz was hit by a serious earthquake in 1989, and the downtown section, which was full of old, unreinforced masonry buildings, was badly damaged. Now, nearly five years later, the cracks and sadness were gone, and the main street buzzed with the latest in espresso bars and New Age cuisine.

Four disgruntled cats met us at Mark's brother's house. We located the front door key, went inside, and served them dinner. We sat down on the living room couch.

"I'm tired," said Mark. He had good reason. After we'd descended to the coast by way of the twisty mountain road, something had gone wrong with the Phoenix One's electrical system. The alternator had failed, and Mark had kept the engine running by using an emergency switch that allowed him to draw power from the coach batteries. It was a serious problem, but one whose solution would have to wait until daylight.

"I'm exhausted, too," I answered. We sat there a while, silent in our weariness. How could we have guessed it would be such a chore to start a new life?

In the last five months, we'd excised ourselves from a routine we'd practiced for twenty years, a way of life we'd known since childhood. It was done in a second, when we pulled out of a driveway in Pasadena, but it had taken a hundred and fifty days to get to that moment.

I was beginning to understand how different our journey was from a trip with a planned itinerary. Those trips have a beginning and an end, a day when you leave, and a day you know you'll go back. We'd had our departure, but we had no back. We had no plan beyond feeding the cats and finding out what was wrong with our alternator. The only other ghost of a scheme was the list we'd made of all the places and people we'd marked on the map we'd hung in the living room of our rented cottage. It was somewhere in the Phoenix, but I couldn't say where.

I'd never taken an open-ended trip before. I'd always planned them out, tied them up neatly before I left with a return ticket or a drop-dead date for being back at work. And now, here I was, a character from a fairy tale. I was going out to seek my fortune, wherever that might take me.

"You know, it's kind of like the difference between Denny's and a greasy spoon," I said out loud. "At Denny's, you look at a slick color menu, and photographs show you exactly what your hamburger will look like. If it doesn't, you can complain. This trip's more like a greasy spoon in a small town. You have no idea what you'll get or who'll be sitting next to you. It may be awful, it may be great. You take your chances. "

"Speaking of greasy spoons," said Mark, "I'm hungry. But I'm too tired to go anywhere." He got up and went into the kitchen. I heard the refrigerator door open.

"You won't believe this," he called. "Lynette left us a home-made pizza. It's all ready to stick into the oven." I smiled. Lynette was a fabulous cook, and somehow, she'd found the time to make us a pizza when she was getting herself and three kids ready to leave for Hawaii.

And so we ate well that first night on the road, and we slept well, too. We needed to. Mark had to find out what was wrong with the Phoenix One's electrical system, and I had a newspaper column to file. I had six days to learn to drive in cyberspace.

RTFM

It's a good thing fax machines came along when they did. They became ubiquitous faster than any technology in the last couple of decades, and they made great training wheels for prospective cyber-surfers. My deal with my editor was that I'd use e-mail to file my columns, but until I could figure out how to do it, he'd accept them by fax.

I was eager to be cutting edge, but because I had no background in Internet technology, culture, or jargon, the easiest way for me to begin to grasp what "online" meant was to pull out one of the free disks America Online had provided me with. I knew about CompuServe, but their "starter kit" cost $20. AOL was already in my hands, and the label said I'd get ten free hours just for trying it. Like thousands and thousands of other would-be cybernauts that year, I took the path of least resistance. I turned on my laptop and slid the disk into its floppy drive.

It didn't work. I installed the software, followed the directions for obtaining a local access number, and logged on. My modem dialed, emitted a stream of static, and beeped. America Online's main menu appeared on my screen, and my cursor metamorphosed into an hourglass. I waited half an hour, but nothing happened. Finally my whole system froze, and I had to shut everything down and start over. I did this seven times.

America Online had a toll-free number to call if you needed help, but even back then, when the membership had yet to break the million mark, you had to wait nearly an hour "on hold." If you were patient enough, you'd finally hear a human voice.

"Hello, this is Robert. How may I help you?"

"When I log onto America Online, I get an interminable hourglass, and then my system crashes."

"What kind of modem do you have?"

"It's an Intel PCMCIA card."

"Well, it should work."

"Well, it doesn't."

"Well, you may need to reinstall Windows."

"Reinstall Windows?"

"Yes. That's all I can suggest."

"Well, OK, I'll try that."

And I did try that, which was tantamount to erasing my whole hard drive. I turned my fancy little laptop into a paperweight in five minutes and a dozen key strokes.

With the help of the consultant from whom we'd purchased the computer, Saint Wes Ferrari, my laptop was restored to functionality. We had to ship the thing to Pasadena, and he sent it back, good as new. My equanimity was also restored, but not before I learned the second of computerland's two golden rules.

The first rule is Back Up, and I had already had enough experience to know its importance. If you're diligent about making extra copies of everything on your hard drive, you really can "back up" if you find you've gone forward a little too recklessly. When I erased my hard drive, I didn't lose anything permanently, not even my high scores in electronic backgammon.

The second rule was new to me: RTFM. RTFM means "Read the F—-ing Manual." The reason the rule is necessary is that nobody wants to do this, and few people ever do. They'd rather call some poor overworked AOL operator who's sick to death of dealing with frustrated non-nerds who don't know a byte from a baud rate. The reason they'd rather wait an hour on hold than read the manual has nothing to do with their ability to obtain information from a written source. It's that prose crafted by a computer wizard is nasty stuff, and slogging through it is worse than a trek though a crocodile-infested mangrove swamp. Really, software manuals are harder to decipher than *Beowulf,* and they put the reader into a worse mood than Grendel's mother's.

Nonetheless, it was RTFM that finally got me online. I'd slip into something comfortable, pour myself a glass of Chardonnay, and read, whether I could understand or not. It was slow, arduous going, but by hook and crook, by bit and piece, by tooth and toenail, I finally clawed out a serviceable metaphor and a working vocabulary for what was going on behind all my pointing and clicking. I'd created my own version of a Frankenstein monster, but it served me well enough to construct gibberish sentences in modem language that allowed it to recognize static, log on to America Online, send and retrieve e-mail, and play trivia in a "chat room." I'd finally entered the nineties, only four years after they started.

I couldn't rest on my laurels. In spite of my progress, I had not achieved the goal I'd had in mind when I started out. A mute black box was still attached by Velcro to the wall above the Phoenix One's desk. I still had no idea how to instruct it to cooperate with my modem and send e-mail via cellular telephone. I tried a dozen times with not even the tiniest shred of success. The machines would hiss at each other, I'd be charged for a call, and no information was exchanged. It would frustrate me so violently that Mark and Marvin would flee any time I suggested I might try again.

I was still using a fax machine to file my stories, and even though I'd come a long way in a short time, I was morose. "I don't think it'll ever work," I lamented to Mark, and no one I asked had any ideas. Even RTFM didn't help. The black box didn't have a manual. And so it sat, mysterious and silent, tantalizing and useless. I needed help before I went bald. Where was a *deus ex machina* when I needed one?

A Cup of Tea and Nothing

From Santa Cruz, we headed north through San Francisco and then west out to the Point Reyes Peninsula. Easterners think California has no seasons, but an unmistakable spring was emerging around us, complete with baby birds and tender green grass.

We stopped at a private campground near the coast. It enjoyed a delightful location along a stream, and was obviously a destination of choice for families on summer vacation. This time of year, however, the grounds were populated by permanent residents and overnight visitors like us.

A man and a woman were inside the office. The man said, "What is that thing?" and pointed through the window at the Phoenix. "I've never seen anything like it, and I thought I'd seen them all." Mark explained, and after we'd signed up for a camping space, he asked if they'd like to see inside. "Sure," they answered in unison, and we trooped out to the parking lot.

"What kind of engine does she have?" the man asked Mark, and the two disappeared under the hood. I invited the woman inside.

"Wow," she said. "Wow. This is my dream. I live here in a trailer, but it doesn't move. I dream of the day I can travel." Her eyes took in everything. "Wow," she said again. "You're really doing it." I showed her the back room, the office. She ran her hand over the desk. "Wow. What a perfect place to write. I'm a writer. I always notice desks."

She fell silent as her eyes traveled from floor to ceiling. She seemed to be memorizing every detail. "Wow," she whispered. "Wow."

Suddenly she gave herself a little shake and said, "Gosh, I'm sorry. I really got lost in my thoughts. Thank you for inviting me in. When you're all set up, why don't you come over to my trailer? We can have a cup of tea." Before I could reply, she added, "I'll come knock on your door in an hour or so." She stretched out her hand. "My name's Cherie, by the way."

True to her word, Cherie arrived at the Phoenix an hour later. We walked across the grass toward a row of trailers. Some were huge and new, some were tiny and old. Cherie's was a little one surrounded by red geraniums and two large propane tanks. It looked as though it hadn't rolled in at least a decade.

Inside was a cozy nest just big enough for one. A cat was curled in an armchair, and every nook was filled with a book or a potted plant. A tiny desk stood near the door, and the tea kettle was beginning to whistle on the two-burner stove. "Do you like almond tea?" she asked. "My favorite," I said.

"I've written a book," said Cherie as she moved the cat and invited me to sit down. "Would you like to see it?"

"Sure," I said, and she opened a box under the desk. She handed me a small volume with a pen-and-ink drawing on the cover. The title was "Nothing."

"Nothing?" I said out loud.

"Nothing," said Cherie, and she laughed. "Yep, it's a book about nothing."

And it was indeed a book about nothing. As we drank our tea, Cherie explained how she'd gotten to a point in her life where she'd lost Everything, which meant, of course, that she had Nothing. "I suddenly realized that Nothing was Something in its own right," she said, "And I started working on the book."

I turned the pages, and the drawings were as important as the words. I sat there, let my tea get cold, and read the whole thing.

"Wow," I said at last. "Wow." It was wonderful.

Cherie and I sat in her little trailer until the sun went down. Two days later, when we left, she said, "Happy Trails!" I never got her last name. I've never seen *Nothing* in a book store.

I like to think that Cherie is on the road somewhere, living her dream. Wherever she is, I'm glad our paths crossed that April afternoon. I'm especially grateful for what she gave me, a cup of tea and Nothing.

·5·

A State Of Amazing Grace

Camping With the Forty-Niners

If you're looking for a real gold mining town of forty-niner vintage, Columbia, California, is the closest you can get. It's tucked into the foothills near Yosemite, and since it never burned completely down or became completely deserted, it never had the chance to become a ghost town.

The cosmetic surgery Columbia has received since it became a state park in 1945 has successfully pickled the main street. It's like a piece of beef jerky, a carefully preserved strip that has lost the juice of its former glory without giving up any flavor. The streets aren't dusty any more, and mad Chinese cooks no longer chase little boys with butcher knives. You have to read about things like that in the visitors' center. Then you can sit on a bench on the sidewalk and chew on the images. Sure enough, the essence emerges, and it's not hard to imagine what it must have been like in the days when the miners lived in tents while they worked feverishly to remove 87 million dollars worth of gold from the hills nearby. You have to look past the yellow school buses and the sign in the candy store window that says, "Only four students may enter at a time." Columbia is the field trip destination of choice for California history teachers, a fact that arouses mixed feelings among the town merchants.

We went to Columbia because Mark had a friend who lived there. "He probably won't be there, because he spends most of his time rafting on rivers in Idaho," Mark explained. He was right. The friend was gone, and we looked in our thick new campground guide to find a place to stay.

"The Mother Lode Trailer Resort sounds pretty good," I said as we headed north away from the town center. I was still getting used to reading the abbreviations and deciphering the icons in the guide. "It seems to have everything we might want." This was well before we learned that the most important things about campgrounds are the ones the guidebooks never tell you.

We soon found ourselves driving into a cluster of buildings that looked more genuinely mining-related than Columbia's mummified main street. "I bet this was a real Gold Rush ranch," said Mark. "Cool."

Mark was ready to award the Mother Lode Trailer Resort an extra star by the time we managed to park. He not only had to use four-wheel drive, he had to do it in reverse up a steep hill. We were teetering off the edge of a fifteen-foot bluff when we were done, and we'd aroused the interest of every other resident in the park. We'd become fast friends with the manager, whose vigorous arm signals narrowly prevented the Phoenix from taking flight.

We settled in, which was still an awkward process for a couple of greenhorns. Leveling the truck required a serious yelling match, and Mark called me a harsh word that wounded my pride. I retaliated with a killing remark and quickly retired inside before I could be broadsided with another salvo of invective. I opened the refrigerator door, and a dozen eggs leapt out and smashed on the floor. I swore. My mood improved, however, when I looked out the window and caught sight of Mark waltzing with a recalcitrant sewer hose. Ah, this is the life, I thought. Free, easy, and above all, romantic.

It was getting dark when we finally sat down to a surly cup of tea. We sipped silently. Suddenly, swelling on the breeze, came a low wail. It got louder. "What is that?" asked Mark. "A sick cow?" Then a melody joined the blend, and, "Bagpipes!" I exclaimed. "'That's 'Scotland the Brave!'" The piper droned his way through three verses and then followed up with the "Skye Boat Song." When he launched into "Amazing Grace," Mark said, "Let's go find out who's behind this."

It didn't take long to find the lungs behind the tunes. They belonged to a retired Puget Sound ship pilot from Seattle who'd even donned a kilt for the occasion. He kept up his highland serenade for an hour or so, invited us to come back the next day for more, and retired to his trailer. The moon had risen by the time Mark and I headed back towards the Phoenix.

As we passed the office, the manager who had so assiduously prevented us from taking a header over the cliff came out to meet us. "I hope the bagpipes didn't bother you," he said.

"Oh, no, of course not," I said. "They may well have saved our marriage."

"Uh, good, I guess," said the manager uncertainly. "The first day he did that, I didn't know whether to applaud him or evict him. Fortunately, nobody has complained. I asked him to keep his concerts early and short." He paused and shook his head. "You have no idea what it takes to manage a place like this," he said. "You have no idea."

Before we left, he invited us to come back later. "I build a campfire every night right out here," he said gesturing toward a large metal ring. "Sometimes we sing, sometimes we tell jokes, and sometimes we just sit and watch the fire."

We thanked him and walked back up to the Phoenix One's perch. I don't remember going to bed or falling asleep, but the next thing I knew, it was morning.

Sanitarium In The Trees

When I woke up, I was still feeling a little glum, in spite of the bagpipes. Real life on real wheels was turning out to be work, and it was straining the adhesive of my marriage. I went outside and sat at the rickety picnic table next to the Phoenix.

"It seems like the only things we ever say to each other are 'excuse me' and 'get out of my way,'" I thought out loud. "We spend all our time bumping into each other."

It was true. The Phoenix is eight-and-a-half feet wide, which means that the available width for movement inside is no more than seven in the widest parts and less than three in the narrowest. There's room to get around, but you have to cancel any feelings you might have about "personal space." I was beginning to feel like I was on a perpetual commute in a Tokyo subway.

Outside, the air was cool and still, and a squirrel scolded me from the branch of an oak tree. "I hate you for bringing that dog!" he screamed. "Hate you, hate you, hate you!"

I sipped my coffee from a stainless steel mug my father had given me. "It'll keep your coffee nice and hot," he'd said. My coffee was stone cold.

I might have wallowed in self-pity for hours, but I was interrupted by the arrival of a tall woman with strong calves and a direct manner. She was walking up the hill with a newspaper, and she stopped in front of me.

"I watched you arrive last night," she said. "That was quite a show."

I smiled weakly. "Glad you enjoyed it," I said. Now go away, I thought.

"Your truck is amazing," she continued. "What is it?"

I told her, and she continued to ask questions. As we talked, my mood rose ever so slightly. "Would you like to come inside?" I asked at last.

"I thought you'd never ask," said the woman. "By the way, my name's Shane." She gave my hand a firm shake.

Shane and I stepped into the Phoenix, where Mark was doing something violent with a pair of pliers and a hose connection. Marvin was thrilled to have a visitor. I showed Shane around.

"Would you like to see my rig?" she asked when I'd finished the tour. People who own RVs always call their vehicles "rigs,'"I was beginning to learn.

"Sure," I said. "Lead the way."

I walked with Shane up the hill, and as we passed other trailers and motorhomes, she started telling me about the permanent denizens of the Mother Lode Trailer Resort.

"That's Cheryl's rig," she said, pointing to a vehicle that was only a little larger than a minivan. "She lives there with a Great Dane, if you can believe it. She used to be a television producer, but she came down with leukemia. She chucked her L.A.

life and came here. She's been in remission a year now."

We continued walking up the road that ran around the perimeter of the grounds. "And that's Don's place," Shane said as we walked by an old silver Airstream trailer. He's lived here forever, or at least since way before I arrived. He's a survivor, too. He lost a leg to bone cancer."

At last we arrived at Shane's "rig," a new-looking motor home with a row of geraniums out front. A woman was watering one of them with a sprinkling can.

"This is Louanne," said Shane. "My roommate."

Louanne, it turned out, was another of the Mother Lode's survivors. She'd been diagnosed with cancer on her thirty-fifth birthday, and had spent the last two years in and out of treatment programs, surgery, and chemotherapy.

"We came here from San Francisco," said Shane. "We'd been here a month before we realized what a sanitarium it is. For whatever reason, this place seems to attract people who need to heal."

I walked back down the hill to the Phoenix, where I could see Mark taking a whack at something on the picnic table with a big rubber mallet. Even from a distance, I could tell he was angry. "What are we doing here?" I asked out loud. "We're not sick."

But then again, maybe we were. Maybe not in the way Cheryl and Don and Louanne were, but somehow in need of solace just the same. Our pipe dream had met reality with a thud. Our rainbow seemed to be ending in a quagmire. We'd dreamed of glorious horizons, but all we were finding were tacks in the road. We stayed at the Mother Lode Trailer Resort for almost two weeks, resting among the oak trees. We took Marvin for long walks in the hills. If we didn't stop bickering, we at least became quieter. The bagpiper played every day at sunset, and Shane came by to chat.

The manager came by, too, nearly every day. He'd noticed our computers, and he had a lot of questions. "How does e-mail work?" he asked. "What's the Internet? What's America Online?"

Finally, I said, "You know, Jim, I can answer your questions, or I can show you. Why don't I show you?"

Virtual Diggings

Jim led me to an old lean-to next to the office. Inside, a chain saw was leaning against one wall, and I nearly tripped over a stack of dusty two-by-fours and a wheelbarrow. Jim pulled the string on a naked lightbulb dangling from a rafter.

"It's not fancy, but there's a desk in here," said Jim. Sure enough, a thick piece of plywood formed a counter across one end of the shed. A leather chair that had once been grand enough for a big city banker sat nearby. "And there's a telephone line."

"Those are the magic words, Jim," I said. "I'll go get my computer."

Twenty minutes later, the light from my laptop's screen bathed two faces in a dim glow. The modem dialed, hissed, and beeped. I'd been navigating in cyberspace for two whole weeks, and suddenly, I was an expert. For an hour, I showed Jim everything I knew about the virtual universe.

Jim was an avid pupil, and by the time we left Columbia, he'd picked my brain clean. He thanked me profusely, but I said, "Jim, I learned as much as I taught."

It was true. There in that Gold Rush shack, I began to see the first glimmer of the tantalizing possibilities the Internet held.

"Can I send a message to someone in another country?" asked Jim. "Does my computer have to be on for them to get it?"

They were simple questions, the same ones being asked by people everywhere that year. The answers were simple, too, but as they steeped in my brain, I began to fathom their profundity. Sitting there in the dusky light, I was an assayer, no different from those who swarmed California in the wake of breathless announcements from Sutter's Mill. My virtual diggings glinted with something more important then fool's gold.

"I love how we're joining the Gold Rush of the nineties in Columbia," I said to Mark. "I've always liked a good metaphor."

"Well, I like metaphors, too," said Mark, "And yes, it's awfully charming. As I see it, though, we're still like the dreamers who never left Ohio. We still don't know how to make that damn black box work with the cellular phone."

The black box, my nemesis. Mark was right. I still hadn't the slightest idea how to get the thing to work.

Loving The Cliff Side

Nowhere in the world have glaciers done a better sculpting job than Yosemite. I heard a Swiss man say once that he didn't want to bother visiting Yosemite Valley because it couldn't be any more beautiful than the Alps. "But the tour I took went there anyway, and I am glad it did. I was awed."

Yosemite is a huge U-shaped bowl carved out of granite by eons of sliding ice. To get inside it, you have to drive over Tioga Pass at the eastern end or across Crane Flat on the west. The weather outside the valley has little to do with what you'll find inside. Yosemite is a separate universe, and its glory varies spectacularly by season.

When I was in college in Southern California, I signed up for a botany class to fulfill a science requirement. It was a great choice, because the professor believed in field trips. One day in October, I joined fifty classmates in a large bus. We headed north for Yosemite, laughing and talking all the way.

The bus crawled up Highway 140 from Mariposa. We were still telling jokes as we approached the summit, still chattering as the bus began its slow descent. Suddenly, the valley opened up in front of us. As a body, we were struck dumb. The valley floor was a rippling sea of brilliant yellow. We had caught Yosemite's maple trees in their brief metamorphosis from green to bare. We spent the weekend in an autumnal wonderland.

"It takes a lot to shut a busload of college students up," I said to Mark as we drove north. "I wonder what we'll find there this time of year." It was late April.

We had driven south from Columbia, and caught Highway 120 west through Chinese Camp. As we gained altitude, snow lurked in the shadows. As we continued to climb, the snow emerged into the sunlight in larger patches. Low ridges of dirty snow lined both sides of the road. "It doesn't look like it's snowed here for a while," said Mark. "This is probably the worst of it."

We crawled on. "Was that a snowflake?" I asked suddenly. "Yes!" I answered myself as a dozen more bounced off the windshield. "It's not like it's really snowing, though," I added. "It's just a tiny flurry. I think it's blowing off the trees."

A dozen more flakes swirled by, and a dozen more. "I hate to tell you this, Meg, but it's really snowing," said Mark. And it was. Snow whirled across our windshield, and now it was sticking to the trees. More and more flakes hit the black pavement in front of us, dancing and sliding and piling up in little drifts.

"It's beautiful," I said as the snow fell softly in the sunlight. And it was. Soon the road was white, and the branches of the fir trees bent down under sparkling coats.

"It's not stopping," said Mark. "And the pattern of the snowfall on the windshield is mesmerizing. I have to concentrate to keep my attention on the road."

I looked ahead. It was dark, even though it wasn't yet two o'clock, and Mark turned on the headlights. The snow was silent, but it was hitting our windshield relentlessly. Caught in our lights, each flake looked like a tiny star, and as we moved forward, it was like driving into a meteor shower.

"Should we stop?" I asked, but it was a stupid question. We were on a two-lane road with no shoulders. A mountain rose on our left, and on our right was an apparently bottomless drop-off. Mark shifted into four-wheel drive, and we pushed on.

The snow formed a thick carpet and crunched under our wheels. We made slow progress. I had long before stopped commenting on the pristine beauty of our surroundings. I was on the cliff side. I wasn't enjoying it.

Suddenly headlights flashed around the curve ahead of us, reflecting on the falling snow. A pickup truck appeared, and, startled, Mark let up on the gas too fast. Because we were in four-wheel drive, this had roughly the same effect as hitting the brakes. The back end lost traction and slid sideways, and the Phoenix, all seven-and-a-half tons of her, slid inexorably toward the truck in front of us. Our headlights lit up the face of its driver. His eyes were all whites, and his mouth was open. He skidded to a stop, and watched in horror as the Phoenix continued on its unplanned trajectory. Six inches short of crushing in his front end, we struck the side of the mountain with a muffled thud.

The driver of the pickup truck quickly regained his composure and his traction and inched around us. I thought we might be permanently embedded in the mountainside, but we backed up easily and continued into the storm. "No harm done," said Mark. "Except to my fingernails," I replied.

We crawled on, and the cliff seemed closer and darker and more threatening at every turn. "What if we'd skidded the other way?" I kept asking myself. But I didn't ask Mark. I knew he would have said, "We're here, aren't we? What's your problem?"

My problem was simple. I was still in the habit of enjoying adventure only as long as it wasn't adventurous. I sighed. "Can't have it both ways," I thought. "It's this or spend the rest of my life at Disneyland pretending. I guess it's time to start loving the cliff side."

Then, and I can't say I was disappointed, the cliff switched to the left, and we started descending. The snow still whirled around us, but the sky was lighter. We continued, and suddenly the sun broke through. The snow vanished, and the valley, clear, green, and lovely, lay before us. "But what's that white down there?" asked Mark. "It almost looks like snow, but . . ."

It was the dogwoods. Bare of leaves, they were covered in delicate, translucent white blossoms. There were hundreds of them scattered across the fresh green meadows, their branches swaying gently in the breeze, their blossoms dancing and shimmering in the sunlight. We stopped. We got out. We stood and looked in silence. Once again, Yosemite had struck its visitors dumb.

The Black Box Speaks

The first thing we saw in Susanville was an elephant. He was standing in a pen by the side of the highway, deftly twirling hay into his trunk and stuffing it into his mouth. He was a small elephant, a teenager perhaps, but still about a thousand pounds of pachyderm more than we expected to encounter outside this Gold Rush crossroads on Highway 395 northeast of Sacramento.

We proceeded down Main Street, and the second thing we noticed was Radio Shack. A franchise electronics store is generally less noteworthy than an elephant, but if you have a mission to make your modem work with a cellular telephone, such places rise in importance.

I'd heard a rumor that Radio Shack had once sold an item called an acoustic coupler, which, as far as I could tell, was basically a hearing aid for a modem. It was a concept I could understand, a refreshing hardware solution to an irritating software problem. I was sick of the silent black box whose idiom defied me. "Let's stop," I said. "If they have an acoustic coupler, we can forget cellular and log on by pay phone anywhere in the world."

We turned left into the parking lot and parked at the back where we could fill up two spaces without causing a traffic jam. As we walked towards the store, Mark said, "I just realized something. My driver's license is about to expire." His fortieth birthday was looming large.

Driver's license renewal strikes dread into the hearts of most Californians. This is because most Californians live in population-dense places, and most of that population seems to spend most of its time waiting in line at the Department of Motor Vehicles, where most of the staff has forgotten how to smile.

"Well, at least you remembered while we're still in California," I said. We were hard on the Nevada border and heading for Oregon. "Otherwise you might have had to qualify from scratch in foreign territory."

"That might be preferable to California DMV purgatory," said Mark, "But now that I've remembered, I might as well do it here."

"Okay," I said, "But first, let's see if we can achieve our grail at Radio Shack."

Actually, the store was called Electronic Butterfly. It seemed to sell all kinds of computer paraphernalia beyond the ordinary Radio Shack lineup. Better and better, I thought. I walked up to the counter where a tall man with a long mustache was taking apart a calculator with a tiny screwdriver.

"Do you sell acoustic couplers?" I asked. The man looked up, startled.

"I think we've got an old one around here somewhere," he said. "But why on earth would you want one?"

He didn't have to ask twice. I poured my heart out. "I want it so I can log on at pay phones as we travel," I said. "I used to want to log on with my cellular phone, but I've given up that dream. I've got this little black box, but . . ."

"A black box?" He interrupted. "What's it supposed to do?"

I explained as well as I could, using every fragment of techno-jargon I could muster. At the time, my fluency in modem-speak was at an all-time high. I'd immersed myself in manuals for weeks. A fair amount had stuck, if only momentarily.

The trouble is, my knowledge was fleeting. I'd detested learning it, and as soon as I could forget it, I did. This means that now, I am incapable of reporting my conversation with anything close to accuracy.

As well as I can remember, it went something like this.

Store clerk: Have you connected your fleeb strut to your crankduff bilgebanger?

Me: Yes, I used the glingbat dub that came with it.

Store Clerk: Good. Then the problem's got to be in the kilber chain. Do you know about kilber chains?

Me: Well, I've been reading the manual. I know how to change them.

Store clerk: Good. Why don't you try changing the jib hammer to a sneak hub and add an X-pod to your huppernog. That may do the trick.

Me: I'll give it a try!

Store Clerk: If the X-pod doesn't work, you can try a Y-frag.

Me: I'll keep it in mind. Thanks!

Mark was so grateful he bought a new battery for his watch even though he didn't need one. "If what you told her works," he said to the clerk, "I'll send you a consulting fee. You may have saved our marriage."

"It's my pleasure," said the clerk. "And don't forget to check your corkle bunt," he added.

"On another topic," said Mark, "Can you tell us where to find the Department of Motor Vehicles?"

The DMV, it turned out, was only a few blocks away, which, come to think of it, was true of everything in Susanville. We went there immediately, and I scribbled what I could remember of the store clerk's advice in my notebook on the way.

"You'll probably be stuck in the DMV for hours," I said to Mark as we parked. "I'll come in with you, but if it's going to take forever, I'll come back out and see whether I can make the black box do my bidding."

The first thing that struck us about Susanville's Department of Motor Vehicles was the size. It was housed behind a tiny storefront and had only one desk. A smiling woman stood behind it, and behind her on the wall was a child's crayon drawing.

"What can I do for you?" she asked cheerily. In five minutes, Mark had a new license.

Five pleasant minutes. Service with a smile. I swear, the next time I'm in Los Angeles and my license needs renewing, I'm driving to Susanville. Even with the twelve hundred mile detour, I'll save time.

As soon as I had the chance, I set up my computer, made the changes the store clerk had suggested, hooked the modem up to the black box, and dialed an access number on the cellular telephone. It didn't work the first time, and it didn't work the second time. The third time — the last time, I told myself — it actually worked. Two pieces of e-mail transferred themselves to my machine. It was hardly earthshaking, but I felt like Archimedes, ready to run through the streets in the buff shouting "Eureka!" Luckily for Susanville, I restrained myself and settled for a celebratory glass of Chardonnay.

Susanville was founded by a man named Isaac Roop, who came to the area in 1854 after he lost his business in a fire and needed a fresh start. He staked his claim along the river, which he named after his daughter. Later the town got her name, too, and grew rapidly into a busy hub for Gold Rush-inspired trade.

That may be Susanville's important history, but for me, this quiet hamlet will always remain a place of marvels: an unexpected elephant, a five-minute driver's license, and, thanks to a friendly Radio Shack genius, a black box with a voice.

At The Feet Of Giants

Technically speaking, it was spring when we arrived in Sequoia National Park, but winter had not wholly retreated. Azaleas were blooming in sunny spots, but the spreading branches of the Presidential Grove's giants preserved a shadowy white carpet at their feet.

We walked quietly among the noble redwoods, each one bearing silent testimony of ancient fires, lightning, wind. In the presence of their extreme age, size and magnificence, I felt like a short-lived nuisance flitting by. How absurd that humans presume to name these beings, to act as though we own them. If

Sequoias had arms, I wouldn't blame them for swatting us.

The first loggers to happen upon a Sequoia grove drooled immediately and put their saws to work almost as quickly. Fortunately, the giants were found lacking in one astonishing regard. They had been blessed with size and beauty and age, but their wood is weak and brittle. Giant sequoias, unlike their smaller coastal cousins, are useless as lumber. A few trees died anyway to serve as side show freaks at Centennial celebrations and world fairs, but giant Sequoias were ultimately worth more alive and standing than sawn to bits.

We may kill them anyway, of course. Sequoias are champions at surviving forest fires, but nobody really knows whether they can survive having their root systems covered with asphalt and pummeled by two million feet a year. Size bears no relation to deadliness, and humans may well be the AIDS virus of the giant redwoods, a lethal invader with a long incubation period.

I hope we're not killers. I hope we're harmless groupies, not death-bearing tsetse flies. I want those redwoods to be here until the sun dies, and as long as I'm here, I want to be able to visit them. They remind me to seize the day.

We walked until the sun began to fade, and then headed for a campground we'd noticed earlier. Campgrounds in national parks have an unwritten rule that every car camper knows. You have to drive by every available site before you pick one. You can't just take the first one, because you might be missing one that's flatter, bigger, shadier, prettier, or just plain better. We began our obligatory circuit, and around the first bend, we surprised six people standing next to a camper laden with mountain bikes. They all wore that now-familiar "What is that thing?" look, and we smiled politely.

The campground was nearly deserted, which made our search more challenging. "That one's got azaleas blooming next to it," I would say. "But that one's got its own water faucet," Mark would counter. "That one's got a view." "That one's nice and level." Before long, we found ourselves back at the entrance gate. "Okay, now we have to pick," said Mark, and we began our second orbit.

This time, the six cyclists were expecting us. They were

standing in a row, and as we rounded the bend, they salaamed in unison, touching their foreheads to the ground in exaggerated adoration. We waved sheepishly, and suddenly a site on the opposite edge of the campground seemed ideal. We fled. The cyclists came by later to make sure we weren't mad. "No, just embarrassed," we said, and Mark spent the next hour happily discussing suspension systems and tag axles.

I retired to my office. From a romance point of view, it was the perfect setting to test the newly functioning black box. I set up my computer and turned on the cellular phone. At last, I thought as I looked at the moon rising above the cedars outside my window, we were truly mobile. At last, location was unimportant. I really could sit at my desk in the wilderness and function just as efficiently as if I were in a Manhattan skyscraper.

The telephone didn't work. In 1994, cellular phones functioned fairly well in major cities and heavily traveled corridors, but relay stations were few in sparsely populated and mountainous regions. I should have known, but my success in Susanville was still fresh.

I wrote for a while anyway, and near midnight, Mark and I went outside to take Marvin for a walk in the starlight. We crunched across the snow and soon arrived at the campground gate. "Look," I said. "There's a pay phone." It was housed in a tidy wooden shelter, and there was a neat cap of snow on its little peaked roof. I could reach out and touch a perfectly functioning telephone, and it was useless to me. And all I want to do is send e-mail, I thought. In 1994, I didn't even know about the World Wide Web. All I wanted was to transmit a small text file once a week from wherever I happened to be. Was that too much to ask? I sighed. I was beginning to think it might be.

· 6 ·

It Makes You Wonder
Whom To Believe

"There's This Guy In A Kayak In Alaska"

There were several forces at work against me in my quest to transmit data on the fly, and the most insidious was the pervasive general belief that millions of people were already doing it. Every single person I talked to seemed to know about someone else who was already doing what I wanted to do. There was a guy in Alaska who logged on from a kayak, a woman on a lemur-watching expedition who sent e-mail from a tree in South America, some guy in Nebraska, some woman in Maine. "Do you have a name? Do you have a number?" I'd ask. No, it was always a friend of a friend. It was the urban legend of the nineties, promulgated by hyperbolic advertising in glossy computer magazines with names like *Portable Computing* and *Mobile Office Solutions*.

Page after page of advertisements touted gadgets and gizmos glowingly described as wireless, and heralded with slogans like "The Ultimate in Telecommuting." Most of these devices were designed for business travelers who stay in hotels. The rest had limited range, or worked only in the middle of Manhattan at high noon. "Oh, sure, we have what you want," salesperson after salesperson would say. Then, within moments, I'd hear, "Our product isn't quite right for you, but there's this guy in a kayak in Alaska. . . ."

Friends sent me flyers from trade shows, clippings from newspapers, brochures from computer stores, but nothing could improve on my black box that the magician in Susanville had brought to life. It worked about one time in five, a frustratingly low average, but so much better than zero, I was grateful. I was also grateful that I had only one writing deadline a week, and that I could still use a fax machine if I had to.

It irked me that the general public had so little understanding of my meager triumph. "Just wait," I said to myself. "Just wait until they want to try it themselves." But nobody seemed to want to. Nobody seemed to grasp the exquisite beauty of being mobile without dropping out of society, of leading a nomadic life without giving up community. "When I travel, I don't want a telephone anywhere near," was the response of people I'd share my dream with. "I travel to get away from things like that." They were talking about vacations. I was talking about my life.

Four years after I first coaxed my black box to speak, the desire for a mobile Internet connection blossomed in a friend of mine. He'd started his own Web site, and he'd finally come to the conclusion that it would indeed be nice to go hiking in the Sierras and still get some work done. This was one of the very same souls who'd been eager to share his certain knowledge of wired kayakers and connected lemur-lovers. With cocky self-assurance, he bought a gadget that was supposed to allow him to log onto the Internet with his hand-held cellular telephone. So confident was he in the legend of mobile access that he didn't even try it out before he left home.

Even in 1998, he was expecting a miracle. He was counting on a cellular telephone with less than one watt of power to find a clean signal in a range of mountains averaging 9,000 feet in elevation. He was expecting his new gizmo to reformat that signal into a package his modem could understand. In addition, he was relying on the whole grand union to stay up and running long enough for him to connect to the Internet, download e-mail, and upload files to his Web site at one-tenth the speed he was used to. "It didn't work because I used the wrong access number," he said.

Maybe so, Captain Video, but do you have any idea how many variables you're dealing with? It's chasing the 99,999 other possibilities that will make you bald. Then again, maybe you're just stupid. After all, there's a guy in Alaska who's been doing it in a kayak since 1994.

The Iguana

Sometimes even I was cowed by the advertising and the omnipresent assumption that mobile Internet connections were yesterday's news. "It's me," I'd think. "I'm missing something obvious."

I'd begin my search once more, only to find that there were no better solutions for our particular requirements available, at any price. You could pay $3,000 for a satellite telephone of the type used on ships, but, in addition to costing $5 a minute to use, they were designed primarily for voice transmission, not data. I knew that the armed forces had been using two-way wireless communications systems for years, but their equipment wasn't available to ordinary mortals.

It wasn't that Mark and I expected mobile communication to be cheap. The black box was expensive to use, too. Since we were constantly moving, we were nearly always assessed "roaming" charges by our cellular service provider. This meant that we paid as much as $5.35 a minute, even if a call didn't go through, and even if the black box failed to perform. Since it often took five or six tries to get the box to work and then four or five minutes once it did, well, do the math. It was expensive.

But wait, I hear you saying. I know there were satellite systems easily available in 1994. That was the year everybody was going in for those little dishes, the portable ones made by RCA. You're right, and they were an instant hit with RV owners. They were reasonably priced, and they provided cable television just about anywhere. In 1994, the satellites could barrage you with images, but you couldn't beam anything back.

And so we were back to the black box, and even in 1998, its direct descendant was still our best choice for coast to coast mobile data transmission. Satellite systems began offering Web access as early as 1996, but they required a land based telephone line to function. Several wireless communications systems appeared on the scene, but they were limited in geographical area.

And here I must mention the acoustic coupler I finally discovered in an ad in a computer magazine, an updated vestige of the Jurassic age of computer technology. "Log on anywhere in the world!" the copy proclaimed. If that included a pay phone in the snow in Sequoia, it sounded good to me. "Hotel phones! Pay Phones! No Problem!" Sold. I ordered one immediately. It came in a little black nylon bag, and when I took it out, its coiled black cord hung down like a tail. "It's a dinosaur that lives today," I said to Mark. "It's an Iguana."

The Iguana was designed to be placed face to face with a telephone receiver and held in place with Velcro bands. You plugged the cord into your modem, and voila! A few other minor adjustments, and you'd be online. Until I actually tried to use it, the Iguana was my Lancelot. After I tried to use it, I realized it would never be my savior. It worked one time in six, and it was stubbornly prejudiced against certain telephone companies. Even so, it was better than no fallback at all, and I kept the little reptile on hand for days when the black box was giving me the cold shoulder.

Death Valley Days

I'd turned forty the December before our house burned down, and now it was Mark's turn. We'd descended to the floor of Death Valley on the big day, and even in May, it's easy to understand why this famous depression has landmarks with names like Furnace Creek, Dante's View and Devil's Golf Course. Native Americans called the valley Tomesha, or "Ground Afire." It's hot at the bottom of the world.

We parked in front of a visitors' center at Furnace Creek, and got out to look around. The sand burned through our shoes, and the sun blazed straight overhead. The air was stiflingly still. Leaving Marvin in the Phoenix with the generator and air conditioning running at full tilt, we stepped inside. Ah. Cool and dark.

Our eyes soon adjusted, and we browsed through the exhibits that explained about the 20-mule teams Ronald Reagan made famous in "Death Valley Days" and the golden age of borax mining. The fact that caught our attention, however, was that ground temperatures in Death Valley can reach nearly 200°F. "Which means you really could cook an egg," said Mark. Today, by contrast, the air temperature was a mere 112°.

"So does that mean nobody comes here in the summer?" we asked the ranger at the desk. "No," he said. "That's the most popular time for German tourists. They come all year round, but they really love the heat.

"The trouble with summer visitors is that they sometimes don't realize they have to take the heat seriously. We go out regularly to scrape desiccated sun worshipers off the road."

I already knew about the love affair Germany has with the sun. I lived in Duesseldorf for two years, teaching at an international school. In a land where drizzly gray skies are the rule, sunny days are rare treasures.

One spring day, I arrived at school to find that classes had been canceled. "Why?" I asked. "Too hot," was the reply. The mercury had risen to a full 80°, and the sky was a brilliant blue. Was it too hot, or too rare a gift to be spent inside? Who cared? The sun had made a rare appearance, and like every other vitamin D-starved soul in Duesseldorf, I stayed outside until dark.

Germans have the reputation of taking more vacations in other countries than any other people in the world. They rarely head north. They go to places with warm sand like the Canary Islands and Rhodes and the Dalmatian Coast. If they're the adventurous sort, they go to Kenya and Egypt and Mexico. The extremists go to Death Valley in August, and stay in places like the Furnace Creek Inn, which for over seventy years has played host to visitors from all over the world.

We found a campground near the Inn that was equipped with electrical hookups. They meant we could operate our air conditioner, which in turn meant that we'd only have to imagine what it was like for the forty-niners and borax miners who passed this way without benefit of Freon. Running at full tilt, our cooling system was able to keep the inside of the coach a few degrees below 90, just cool enough to leave Marvin inside while we went exploring.

We stuck to the shade of a row of tamarisk trees and soon found ourselves at the edge of a swimming pool. Bobbing listlessly in the pool, looking like the floating remains of a shipwreck, were two lobster-red men and one scarlet woman. Beached lifelessly around the pool were more crimson bodies in bathing suits. Heat waves rose in shimmering little eddies off the concrete deck.

"If I didn't know better, I'd say we were looking at the aftermath of murder by blowtorch," I whispered to Mark. "I'd bet money they're from someplace cold, trying to soak up enough rays to last them through a northern winter. A man lying on an air mattress sneezed. "Gesundheit!" said the woman next to him. "They're alive!" said Mark. "They're German!" I said at the same time.

We decided to act like snakes instead of Northern Europeans and stay inside until dark. We returned to the Phoenix, where the air conditioner was doing an admirable job. Our thermometer read 82°.

"Well, it's your birthday," I said to Mark. "What do you want to do to celebrate?"

"How about a game of backgammon to start with?" he said, and I rummaged in a cabinet to find the set.

Twenty minutes later, Mark said, "The sky looks weird." He was right. It was yellowish green. We went outside, where it was still as hot as a blast furnace, and there was still no hint of a breeze. "It looks even weirder now," I said.

"Look over there," said Mark. Beyond the tamarisk trees, an opaque yellow wall was moving in our direction. We could see the mesquite in the distance begin to bend and snap before they were obliterated by the advancing cloud. A few minutes later, we felt the first gusts of wind.

We retreated inside the Phoenix. Mark closed all the windows and raised all the shades. We watched the billowing mass approach, and soon we were enveloped in a cloud of sand and dust. Visibility shrank to zero, and we could hear the dry grit scour the outside of the Phoenix.

"I'm going outside," said Mark. "I'm staying here," I replied. Mark left, admitting a flurry of sand in the process. Five minutes later, he was back. "It's suffocating out there," he panted. "It's like being inside a vacuum cleaner bag. I couldn't breathe."

The storm lasted about an hour. I'd been in blizzards before, and thunderstorms complete with serious wind, but this was the first wholly arid tempest of my life. "If we'd put a steak out there, we'd have jerky now," I said. "Oh, and happy birthday, Mark."

"Best one yet," he said.

The Jayhawkers

We left the campground before dawn the next morning. Everyone in the place knew it, because it's impossible to sneak in the Phoenix One. When you turn the ignition switch, it emits a roar reminiscent of an Apollo rocket achieving liftoff. When you turn on the headlights, every object within a hundred yards is illuminated to the level of high noon. Since it couldn't be silent, we made our exit swift.

We made it to Zabriskie Point in time to see the sun rise over its other-worldly clefts and wrinkles. We rose high to Dante's View and scanned the inferno before the sun burned the cool morning breeze away. By ten a.m. we descended into Badwater, at 265 feet below sea level, the lowest bit of dry land in the continent.

A big red double-decker bus had beaten us to the spot, and two dozen tourists were busily taking pictures of the sign marking sea level high above them. The bus's front end looked like an ordinary touring coach, with recliner seats and tall tinted windows. The back end was different. It sported two rows of porthole-like windows.

"I think they sleep in there," said Mark. "Those look like berths." We moved closer for a look, and he was right. It was a camping-mobile, and it amazed us. While we should have been marveling over the unique little fish that survive in Badwater's ponds, and letting the alien topography overwhelm us, we found ourselves wondering why tourists would pay for the privilege of sleeping eighteen inches away from a stranger with smelly feet. "They should just sign up for a tour of duty on a submarine," said Mark.

The red buses, we discovered later, are very popular with European tourists. They spend twenty-one days traveling, and they do most of their own cooking. If they aren't friends before they begin, they are when they're done. "Either that or they're dead," said a driver we met at a hot springs resort. "And I'm dead regardless."

Before retiring for the hot part of the day, we stopped once more at the visitor's center in Furnace Springs. "We've heard about the Jayhawkers," we told the ranger. "And we'd like to learn more." We left with the book that would not only tell us the story of the intrepid band of gold-seeking Midwesterners who were on the spot when Death Valley received its name, but also the beginning of a tradition of our own. I read *The Jayhawkers* aloud as we drove. Since then, we've never been without a "road read," a work from the great corpus of travel literature that begins with Homer's Odyssey and won't end until the last adventurer reaches the horizon.

The Jayhawkers was a perfect beginning. It was the history of a group of forty-niners who left Illinois in 1849 hoping to reach California's gold fields before winter. Well-equipped with wagons, oxen, and supplies, they had every expectation that their journey would go smoothly.

It did, until they left Utah. A map surfaced to challenge the knowledge of their Mormon guide, and there was dissent among the wagons. The group split up, some trusting the guide, and some electing to follow the new map.

Instead of leading them on a shortcut, the map led the travelers into Tomesha. The name Death Valley is the Jayhawkers' legacy, and the fact that many of them lived to tell the story of their agonizing ordeal in the Amargosa Desert bears witness to their stamina and determination.

People nowadays use the Gold Rush as a metaphor for the mad stampede into cyberspace that exploded in 1996. It's natural to compare the millions who rushed to stake claims on the electronic gold fields to the fortune seekers who converged on California in 1849. But the Web Rush took place on a plane where thirst is virtual, and dying oxen are mere metaphor. The bones in Death Valley exist in three dimensions, hard evidence that the Jayhawkers and their ilk gave their dream everything they had.

Adventure In Finding Out

From Death Valley, we headed north out of the arid rain shadow and into lush coastal spring. The roads were lined with lupines, and as we drove farther north, purple and white foxgloves. At the north edge of California, we slowed down to wend our way through the primeval groves of Redwood National Park. Nearby, we stopped in Scotia, last of the company towns and home of the largest redwood mill in the world.

"We're trying to get more land for the park," said the park ranger, "Before all the virgin forests are gone."

"Trees are a renewable resource," said the lumber mill guide. "We plant more than we cut." And so the struggle goes. Coast redwoods and the silent fern kingdoms over which they reign are beautiful. Coast redwoods make beautiful houses.

On up into Oregon we drove, to the center of the state. All our lives we'd heard of Crater Lake, and now, even though the snow was still thick on the mountains, we wanted to see the legendary waters.

White men had been trapping in the Cascades for fifty years before any of them knew about the lake in the high caldera. They did business with Indians who knew the place well, but not a one divulged the secret. The lake was sacred.

It wasn't until 1853 that John Wesley Hilman and a band of prospectors who were searching for the Lost Cabin Gold Mine stumbled upon this unrevealed marvel. Their initial reaction is unrecorded, but I like to think they were struck dumb when they reached the rim and first looked upon the deep blue lake created when Mount Mazama exploded over seven thousand years before.

We were speechless, and so was the rest of the crowd of spectators that had gathered to look down into the serene circular crater that holds water nearly two thousand feet deep. There were hundreds of people there on that chilly spring day, and we were all moved to silence. Even the little boy next to me whispered as he pointed out Wizard Island to his mother.

The road around the lake was still snow-covered and impassable, so our view on that pristine day was limited to what we could see from the parking lot. We stood looking until the ice under our feet made itself felt through our shoes. Then we headed back to the Phoenix.

As we approached, a man stepped out of a sleek black car and greeted us. "Is that your truck?" he asked. "It's quite the ride."

Mark answered his laundry list of questions about suspension and horsepower and mileage and torque, and then I said, "Where are you from?"

"New Jersey," he replied, "I'm the guy people call when they have too much money."

And so began a conversation of a type to which we've since become accustomed. When you meet people on the road, away from home, out where everyone's a stranger, they want to tell you stuff. They want to tell you whatever it is they can't talk about back where it matters. Maybe they want to strut a little. Maybe they want to unload. Whatever else may be the case, they want to talk.

The man from New Jersey wasn't kidding, he said. He really was the guy to call if you had too much money. He dealt in money, great piles of it, mountains of coins, bales of bills. "Cash piles up in places like Las Vegas and Atlantic City. It piles up in banks. Have you ever thought about what happens to it all?" We hadn't. "Well, it comes to people like me in huge unmarked trucks. You'd never in a million years guess they were carrying money. We sort it, weigh it, redistribute it. And if it's old, we burn it."

He went on about the vast quantities of coins and bills he dealt with. "It's beyond ordinary comprehension," he said. "Millions and millions of dollars pass through our facility every day. Every single day. You can't even imagine the kind of security arrangements we have. It's more elaborate than Fort Knox, and nobody really knows about it." Finally Mark asked, "Where, exactly, is this place?"

The man fell silent. His cheeks turned a little redder than the chilly breeze had made them. "Gee, uh, I can't tell you. I've already told you too much." He was running our conversation back through his brain, scanning it for dangerous details that might now be out of the bag. "Really, I'm sorry, I don't know what I was thinking," he stammered, and then he vanished into his car.

It's easy to think you're away from it all when you're three thousand miles from home and standing on the edge of a volcanic lake. What harm can come from telling a story to a couple of strangers? It feels good to wow them, and it's such a pleasure to get the chance to speak freely about secret things. Then, the question. "Where, exactly, is this place?" You'd better leave fast. It's either that or kill them.

More often, it's tall tales that come out of the mouths of strangers on the road. We met a man in Morro Bay, California, who claimed he'd sailed his little sloop to Hawaii, and that in a matter of weeks he'd be taking her "around the Horn." The little sloop looked as though it had never been past the breakwater, and the man's story had the cadence of oral tradition, a well-rehearsed epic aged in a whisky keg and roasted over slow cigars. It lived only in the telling.

Sometimes, though, you just can't tell. A hunter in a campground in Montana held us in thrall with a story of industrial intrigue. You'll have to decide for yourself whether it's fact or fantasy.

"I was working in an exclusive hunting lodge in the early eighties. One week, a small coterie of top Coca-Cola executives rented the whole place so they could have it to themselves. I was sort of their valet during the day, the guy who made sure they had pencils and coffee and overhead projectors — whatever they wanted all day long. They spent most of the day meeting together in one room, and I was pretty much with them all the time.

"At first I didn't pay much attention to what they were talking about. I'd been working at the lodge for nearly a year, and we had executive groups coming all the time for retreats and conferences. Mostly they talked about stuff an outsider wouldn't be interested in.

"But these guys were different. They were talking about Coke itself. Coke was sweetened with cane and beet sugar, and the price was rising at an alarming rate. They wanted to switch to corn syrup, which was much cheaper. The trouble was that corn syrup tastes different— not a lot different, but different enough that if you tasted the two right next to each other, you could tell easily.

"So basically, these guys were trying to figure out a way to get Coca-Cola off the shelves for about two months. That way, people wouldn't be able to compare the old with the new. So you know what they came up with? New Coke! They spent that week planning how they'd make a new recipe for a new-and-improved Coke, and they'd put it out there and take old Coke off the shelves.

"They were pretty sure everyone would hate New Coke. They'd advertise it for two months, field all the press, then admit failure and bring back original Coke. Of course, it wouldn't be totally genuine, the new old Coke would be sweetened with corn syrup, but by then there wouldn't be enough real old Coke to compare it to. And of course, if by some miracle New Coke was a hit, they'd just keep the new recipe.

"By the end of the week, they'd pretty much thought of every detail, including which one of them would be the public whipping boy for the whole orchestrated fiasco. He'd leave in shame, but he'd be getting a pretty fabulous golden handshake on his way out.

"So that was pretty much it, and the group left. Six months later, I watched the whole thing unfold exactly as they'd planned. It was brilliant. Nobody ever suspected a thing."

"I sure didn't," I said. "I've never even heard anyone mention the possibility of subterfuge. And New Coke has become the textbook example of corporate marketing failure."

"I know," said the hunter, smiling. "It makes you wonder who to believe, doesn't it?"

When you live on the road, you spend a fair amount of time wondering whom to believe. Do you believe the directions you get from a gas station attendant when they directly contradict your map? Do you believe a sign that says "Road Not Safe for RVs?" Do you believe that if you take a tiny road out of Wallace, Idaho, and go up past Burke, Mace, and Cornwall, through Yellow Dog, Black Bear, Frisco and Gem, cross a rickety wooden bridge so narrow your tires barely fit on the planks, and drive up a rocky track to the top of Shifter's Hill, that you'll find a man hard at work with a chainsaw? The trouble with not believing is that you'll miss meeting Vern Pine, a sculptor of consummate talent who creates masterpieces with power tools.

It's not safe to believe the gas station man. It's risky to ignore the sign. You never know when a sagging bridge will plunge to the river below, and who's to say whether the chainsaw master up on Shifter's Hill is an artist or a madman? There's safety in wondering. There's adventure in finding out.

· 7 ·

Closed Until The Verdict Comes In

Making Money On The Road

When we first went to Traveland, the Revcon Trailblazer didn't just attract our attention. It riveted it. It nailed us to the floor and refused to let us go. It ignited a firestorm of feelings best reflected in cliches. Life's an adventure. The world is our oyster. It was only a motorhome, but it absolutely screamed the call of the open road.

Once we were behind the wheel, we immediately began to notice that the Phoenix had the same effect on lots of people. Not everyone harbors a secret longing to hit the road, but Jack Kerouac and John Steinbeck are the tiny tip of an enormous iceberg. We quickly came to recognize the faraway look that would steal into a young man's eyes as he ran his hand over the hood. "I'm going to do this," he'd say. "Some day." There were dreamers everywhere, would-be itinerants who longed to leave the baggage of life behind and head for the horizon.

I myself was once an Easy Rider romantic, longing for a trip that would reflect in three dimensions the journey of life. I've always been a lover of metaphor, and there is no better allegory for human existence than odyssey. In the dreaming stage, it's easy to forget that life on a roll is not all sunsets and singing Bobby McGee. In the dreaming stage, it's literature, a mighty epic, a noble saga. Nothing happens without divine meaning. It's a perfect composition. It's freedom. It's nothing left to lose.

You write the book before you leave. You're Homer, you're Bunyan, you're Twain. Really, the journey is far more magnificent before you set tire to pavement. As soon as you do that, as soon as reality bites, you're wrestling a sewer hose and agonizing over how to pay for another tank of gas. It's the part the authors who've inspired you left out, or if they mentioned it, they couched it in heroic terms. Trust me, there's nothing epic about thawing out fifty gallons of frozen sewage with a diesel flame thrower. Heroic dialogue does not include lines like, "There's a big hard turd clogging the hose."

But the sunsets are poetry in action, and with the windshield wiper slapping time, you still get the chance to sing. It's time for a new dream to kick in, and there's an excellent one ready and waiting. It's the dream of making money on the road.

The basic theory to which most of America subscribes is that unless you're Charles Kuralt, making money on the road means picking oranges or cleaning restrooms or selling rocks or singing country songs in rundown road houses. Variations on those themes are pretty much the price you have to pay for getting to be Easy Rider. If you want the big bucks, you have to settle down, wear panty hose and be happy with two free weeks a year.

That's the view from a high-rise, anyway. To make the dough, you gotta pay the price. But wait! You say you're out there all the time? Always on the road? By George, you could be selling something! I never cease to be amazed how many times this thought strikes a member of corporate America like a lightning bolt. He's always positive he's the first one to come up with such a brilliant notion.

Because this particular flash hits so often, the number of sales opportunities which have been presented to us is correspondingly large. With proper motivation, we could be raking in cash right this second hawking cosmetics, vitamins, hand-made baskets, motorhomes, tires, bee pollen supplements, memberships to campground clubs, emergency road service plans, magazines, RV equipment, and pre-paid legal insurance plans, to name just a few. There's nothing particularly wrong with a one of them, except maybe the baskets, which had the sad look of a sweatshop about them. For a while we did carry brochures and videos about Revcon Trailblazers, but the company was mysteriously lackadaisical about following up on leads.

But no "business opportunity," no selling scheme, no money-making program outdoes that constant of the get-rich movement, pyramid marketing. Before we left town, a man we hardly know made an appointment to see us. "Just want to run something by you," he said. I already had my suspicions, and they were instantly confirmed when he arrived with tapes, books, brochures and videos.

"I was thinking that if you're going to be on the road, you might be interested in selling something," he said with the smug assurance of someone who knows he's had an original thought. "Let me tell you about my company."

His company had a catalogue full of jewelry and china and wooden boxes and "collectable" statuettes. "It's so perfect for you," he said. "You don't have to worry about inventory." Unfortunately, there was nothing in the whole scheme we did want to worry about.

Later, when e-mail was becoming more universal, and the explosion of interest in the World Wide Web had begun, we received an e-mail message from a man in Dallas. He'd discovered *RoadTrip America*. "What a neat idea!" he wrote. "Have you ever thought about the fact that you're in a perfect position to be selling something?"

Resisting the urge to write back something like, "No, we specialize in original thoughts," Mark replied politely. As we neared Texas, Bill's messages arrived with increasing frequency, and included tempting remarks like, "I'd love to meet you, and I'd love to have the chance to introduce you to some business associates of mine. We're all fascinated by what you do."

Flattery has always been a wonderful sales technique, and we fell for the bait. When we arrived in Dallas, we arranged to meet Bill at the high-tech hub known as the Crystal Palace. It's the home of Sony and Microsoft and AT&T Wireless, but we were headed for the offices of something I shall hereafter refer to as E-Z-Bux.

The owners of E-Z-Bux had invested in a lavish spread. We were met at the door by Bill and a sidekick wearing tight jeans and high-heeled cowboy boots. "Welcome y'all," they said. We exchanged hearty handshakes, and stepped into a plushly carpeted receiving area full of unopened boxes and new desks.

E-Z-Bux had just opened, they said. It was a ground floor opportunity in the exciting new world of electronic communication. "We offer a product that can double, triple, and even quadruple, a person's efficiency and productivity. Every man, woman, and child in the country is going to be screaming for it, and our marketing plan makes it an exciting opportunity for anyone who joins us now."

Bill paused and turned to the sidekick, as if to say, "Take it away, Hopalong!" The cowboy rose to the occasion, and for fifteen minutes attempted to describe just what this remarkable device was. By ignoring his lavish use of phrases like "high-tech platform" and "bleeding edge," we soon divined that the product they were pushing was gussied-up voice mail. But the cowboy, whose penchant for hyperbole was equaled only by the size of his belt buckle, wasn't nearly as excited about the voice mail as he was about the "real opportunity," the chance to "share his discovery" with the clambering masses.

In case you're one of the lucky minority who has yet to enjoy the pleasure of being on the receiving end of this kind of sales pitch, let me help you out in advance. If someone says they have "an opportunity to share," you can forget about laundry detergent or vitamins or voice mail. What they're really after is giving you the privilege of memorizing their routine and spouting it off to any poor soul you can hogtie for an hour. The product is only an excuse to mine human avarice, to promote the tempting possibility that there really is a trick to earning buckets of money without lifting a finger.

"And you're in the perfect position to achieve success," Bill was saying. "You're out there, on the road, meeting new people every day. Have you ever thought about what a great opportunity you have?" We fled.

But don't get me wrong. Mark and I were avidly interested in pursuing business that would both keep us on the road and dovetail seamlessly with life in motion. We just had our standards, and we were not willing to clip our dreams to fit the prevailing notion that nomads are bottom feeders, and that the price of being Odysseus is professional groveling.

Flavor Beyond the Cup

From Crater Lake we headed to Bend, then west to the coast and north through Portland to Washington. Lots of Seattle natives were eager to tell us they don't like coffee, and that the espresso epidemic was the result of evil spores that blew up from California. California was the whipping child for every ill Seattle was suffering, but in the case of coffee, the blame seemed ill-placed. Washington had more caffeine entrepreneurs than Italy. The carts were everywhere, and for a java lover like me, it was terrific. It was impossible to get more than two steps away from a friendly espresso maker.

I can't understand how Seattleites delude themselves into thinking their coffee phenomenon is California's fault. They can't avoid claiming Starbucks as their own, and it has become the McDonald's of the cappuccino crowd, invading rejuvenated downtown shopping enclaves across the land and infecting the vernacular with nearly as many new words as the computer revolution. I don't know whether to laugh or cry when I hear Mark order a "double tall skinny latte." He can voice the phrase in Memphis or Malibu, and get just what he wants. So can lovers of "grande easy whip percent mochas." Every time I go inside a coffee establishment of the new order, I hear another idiom. The old argot of diners may have perished, but hello, java joint jargon.

I soon came full circle with the coffee explosion. When we first got to Seattle, I reveled in the ubiquity of espresso. When we left, I noticed that the farther we separated ourselves from the caffeine capital, the harder it was to find what I considered good coffee. "It's like New York bagels," I said to Mark. The farther you get from Manhattan, the less likely you are to find a real one." This line of thinking led me to the sad image of a small town in Kansas. I imagined its welcome sign: "Welcome to Dead Center, where the coffee is awful, and the bagels are frozen."

It was true in 1994 that good coffee was pretty much a phenomenon of the far west, and a fresh bagel could only be found in the shadow of the Empire State Building. By 1998, things were different. Bagels were the new jelly donut, and Starbucks had swept the land. Two more regional wonders had hit prime time, and were enjoying the heady status of mass marketing and mob consumption. Just like pizza in the seventies, java and bagels were set to usher in the new millennium.

"It's one more example of the loss of regionalism in America," we might lament. "Bad coffee has gone the way of local dialect. The good old days are dead." I am sometimes surprised by my own nostalgia for a cup of boiled brown branch water served in a thick mug on a chipped Formica counter. But I have nothing to fear. Real American coffee is alive and well. I find it waiting patiently on back burners everywhere, right next to the glass cases full of Danishes. More than once, Mark and I have chosen to slip into a familiar tuck-and-roll Naugahyde booth, even when there was a Starbucks right next door. Flavor goes beyond the cup.

But I digress. And coffee wasn't the first thing we noticed when we drove into Seattle. The Space Needle was. There it stood, rising above Puget Sound, reigning over the city that airplanes built. It's hard to think of a prettier urban landscape than the view that greeted us when we drove into Seattle from the south. Mount Rainier hung like a mirage in the distance.

We'd heard that Boeing gave factory tours. We'd just finished watching cheese production on a grand scale in Tillamook, Oregon, and I was hot to see a 747 roll off the assembly line. By great good fortune, the whole city had gone airplane mad the week we arrived, because Boeing was unveiling the first jet ever to be completely designed on a computer before it was built. The first test flight of the new 777 was only days away.

Boeing And The O.J. Effect

Having heard that the world shows up for the Boeing factory tours, we rose early and drove to Everett, home of the biggest building in the world, if you measured by volume. Inside, the biggest commercial aircraft in the world were being assembled, dozens at a time. Even though the sun was barely above the horizon, we were not the first. A Canadian couple was already waiting by the door. A sign said that tour groups would be limited to forty people. The line soon grew to twice that, but nobody left.

Eventually, a man in a suit and a clip-on name tag unlocked the door from the inside. "We can accommodate everybody," he said cheerfully, and he led the way to an auditorium where, thanks to the wonders of time-lapse photography, we watched a 747 get assembled in seven minutes.

At last it was time for the real thing, and we rode a bus to the giant building. Inside, nearly a dozen 747s were in various stages of assembly. We watched from a high platform, and the guide yelled explanations over the reverberation of ten thousand power tools.

Later we went outside to see new planes getting their final touches before delivery. Each one is fitted on the inside according to the buyer's desires, and the exterior decoration is custom-tailored, too. "The buyers have to choose between an all-over paint job, or leaving a lot of silver showing," said the guide. "The paint adds a lot of weight, but the naked metal takes more maintenance. They pretty much have to decide whether they want to spend money on extra fuel or extra labor."

Before we left, we caught a glimpse of the new 777, which had yet to take to the sky. It was smaller and sleeker than the 747, and sported only two engines. "But look at those engines," said Mark. "Each one is bigger around than a DC10." It was true. The 777 was powered by a couple of monsters.

Boeing was like the redwoods. When we saw the whole operation, everything was huge, so everything looked reasonably sized. But then I started thinking about how a 747 would look parked in front of a house. You'd have to install a giant sequoia in the front yard to balance it out.

We retired to Bothell, a suburb north of downtown Seattle. It was late spring, and the largest flock of Canadian geese in the universe had touched down in the campground, which had a pond. They were so large and so aggressive that Marvin wouldn't go outside. Geese are high output birds, and this meant we didn't want to go outside either. We were hostages in the Phoenix.

It didn't matter much, because it was an afternoon when most of America was being held hostage to breaking news in Southern California. A white Bronco was leading the Los Angeles Police Department on a slow tour of the freeway system.

That slow chase knit the backdrop of our travels for the

next fifteen months. We watched the opening ceremonies in Seattle, and thousands of miles and millions of tabloid headlines later, we watched the Fryeburg Fair, Maine's oldest and most popular county fair, shut down for the finale. The vendors stopped hawking, the lumberjacks stopped chopping, and even the office put out a sign that read "Closed Until The Verdict Comes In."

The three-ring coverage of O. J. Simpson's murder trial permeated every state and oozed into Canada. There was no escape. It blanketed the continent better than a flock of super geese, and the newscasters served it up as daily manna across the land.

Flying Penguins

It was time to call Charlie. We'd never met him before, but we were pretty sure we'd like someone who spends all his time making juggling toys shaped like penguins and cows and tomatoes and killer whales. Back when Wizards of Wonder was a going concern, we'd sold Charlie's products. A number of crates of them had gone up in smoke.

Mark had managed to grab a file that contained a list of our suppliers as he fled the fire, and he'd written letters to each one explaining what had happened and asking what we owed. The response was heartening. Companies wrote, saying things like "Take as much time as you want to pay." Some even telephoned. Charlie Brister sent a letter on Flying Penguini stationery. "Come see us if you're ever in Seattle," he wrote.

We'd warned Charlie we were on our way, and his response was still warm. "You can come by our factory," he said. "We'll give you a tour."

Charlie reiterated his invitation over the telephone, and the next morning we headed for Chasley, the name of the company begun ten years before by Charlie's wife Barb, a world-class juggler and the creative force behind the company's products. "Two factory tours in two days!" exclaimed Mark. "This is terrific!"

When we arrived, Charlie was juggling lobsters outside the front door. We followed him inside, where a poster announcing our visit was pinned to a bulletin board, and the entire staff was expecting us. It was clear from their faces that they didn't quite know why. "Who are these people?" they seemed to be dying to ask. "And why in the world are we caring about their arrival?"

Charlie didn't care what they thought. He gave us a tour worthy of royalty, showing us every step in the evolution of a small cow destined to be part of a threesome that was packaged in a milk carton and labeled Milkshake, "because that's what you get when you juggle a trio of Holsteins," said Charlie. We saw how white fabric was cut and screened with a pattern of black spots. After it was sewn together, each cow was stuffed with crushed walnut shells. "We tried lots of stuffing materials," explained Charlie, "Sand, beans, millet— but they were all the wrong size or the wrong weight. Juggling toys have to feel right, and walnut shells have turned out to be the best filler we've found." After we saw how the cows were packed into their cartons and readied for shipping, Charlie took us out to lunch at a nearby sandwich shop, where, no surprise, espresso coffee was available, too. While we ate, Charlie regaled us with Bill Gates legends, which were already rampant in Seattle in 1995.

Before we left, we'd discovered that Charlie and his family lived in Bothell, which was the same neighborhood where our goose-infested campground was. We explained the hazards and invited them over for dinner. "Don't wear your party shoes," we said.

We gained four new friends that day, and I learned something that at the time seemed profound. If you discounted magnitude, there wasn't a whole lot of contrast between Boeing and Chasley. They both had tidy assembly lines and interchangeable parts. They both made flying things that required skill to use. They both gave terrific factory tours. Well, actually there was one difference. Boeing didn't give out samples.

Cruising

One of the reasons we'd headed for Seattle in the first place was that we had reservations on a Princess Cruise to Alaska. Yes, a Princess Cruise, a lavish one that featured enormous ice sculptures and great pallets of food and giant shakers of piña coladas and classes in how to fold napkins. If motorhomes had seemed foreign to me, cruises like this one were as alien as flying saucers.

It wasn't that I hadn't traveled by ship before. As a child,

I'd voyaged from New York to Panama on the USS Gibbon when my father was tapped to become military attache to Costa Rica. Three years later, we'd returned on the USS Geiger, with stops at San Juan, Puerto Rico, and Guantanamo Bay, Cuba, before we climbed to the highest deck to watch for the Statue of Liberty through the fog. Because my father was the highest ranking non-crew officer on both ships, we were handled with kid gloves. It was on the first of those journeys that I learned what VIP meant. "You are one," said my father. "Enjoy it while it lasts."

I've since traveled by ship in Europe, on beautifully appointed crafts that plied the waves between Venice and Alexandria. Even the ferries that called at the ports on the Dalmatian Coast were quite lovely, especially the VIP lounges and dining rooms that first-class tickets afforded.

But the Love Boat was something else entirely. A trip on a ship like this was cruising for cruising's sake, with a "because you've earned it" attitude and a battalion of full-time masseuses. We'd made a leap to reconcile ourselves to the fact that we were now members of the Winnebago crowd we'd held in disdain, but a chasm separated us from Princess Cruisers. Heretofore, we'd considered cruises to be something for soft wimps who wanted to travel but didn't want to leave home, who wanted to see the world, but not smell it, touch it, or taste it.

So why were we packing our bags and abandoning Marvin at a kennel in Seattle for a float through the Inland Passage? The main reason was that some friends were celebrating their twenty-fifth wedding anniversary by taking this cruise, and they'd decided it would be more fun if they brought a party along. The second reason was that we were still fire crazy, which meant that we still peppered our conversations with questions like "What have we got to lose?" One thing we had to lose was money, of course, but we had some at the moment, and "What the heck?" won out. We would soon be winging our way to Anchorage and catching a big white boat in Seward.

Our haughty disdain for cruise ships and their clientele vanished as we sank into the sybaritic luxury of the Regal Princess, the newest and fanciest craft in the Love Boat fleet at the time. Seduced by the perfectly-orchestrated week-long performance of a crew of thousands, we ate enough to power a chain gang for a month and washed it down with an ungodly amount of fruit-diluted alcohol. We enjoyed the quintessential cruise experience, perfect to the last bite of baked Alaska. It was easy to ignore the conveyor belt feeling while we were being so thoroughly indulged, but I came away with the distinct impression that unless your ship hits an iceberg, one cruise is pretty much like another.

Mark and I spent a lot of time on the top deck, where we made friends with Craig and Susan, a couple of Canadians with an unending supply of jokes we hadn't heard. From our perch, we saw eagles, dolphins and whales. One day, when the ship drew near land, we even saw bears. Because we were cocooned in luxury, we had to keep reminding ourselves it was all real. For all the genuine contact we had, we might as well have been watching a National Geographic video on a really big television.

So have we really been to Alaska? I felt like I was really there the first night, when we stayed in a hotel in Anchorage. It was the summer solstice, and the sun never set. Men in waders fished all night in the river outside our window, pulling salmon after salmon out of the water. The feeling returned the sunny morning that the Regal Princess pulled into Glacier Bay. The sky was so clear we could see for miles, and skyscraper-sized shards of ice broke off the face of the glacier, falling down to the sea in a roar of "white thunder." Beyond those two riveting scenes, I've had only a postcard view of that wonderful wilderness, a peek from an incongruous lap of luxury with comfortable beds and gigantic refrigerators. Being a VIP felt good, but the insulation had its price.

Not long after we returned to Washington, the couple whose anniversary we'd celebrated announced that they were getting a divorce. "So much for the Love Boat," said Mark. We were driving up Whidbey Island, on our way to the Olympic Peninsula. The scenery was achingly lovely, and a soft breeze blew over new grass on rolling hills. Purple foxgloves lined the road.

We should have been happy. We'd just returned from the kind of cruise that makes a winning game show contestant delirious with joy. We were pursuing our own dream of living on the road. We were driving through paradise in the world's snazziest motor home.

And we were fighting.

· 8 ·

"To Fight No More Forever"

Trouble in Paradise

Yes, we were fighting. We bickered over where to go, what to eat, how to drive. It mattered not that beyond our windows lay the Olympic Peninsula, that glorious amalgam of geographical extremes. It made no difference that snow-capped Mount Olympus towered over us, the gods' New World aerie. We were impervious to divine influence, bent only on hurling verbal sticks and stones. Surrounded by splendor, we responded with a whine.

It was high-contrast proof that psychic baggage is hard to lose. You can't set it down in an airport and wait for the bomb squad to dispose of it. You can't leave it out with the trash. You can drive a thousand miles, believing all the way that you left your heart in San Francisco, but danged if you don't find it still stuck on your sleeve in Tacoma.

I don't know why we fought. The answer is as elusive as the reason the world had to explode just because one Archduke got assassinated. Dominoes fall. Wars happen. Maybe it was because inventing a new life is hard. Maybe you get bellicose when your assumptions are shattered. In any event, life isn't all lush valleys, and we'd clawed our way to the other extreme. We languished in our own private intemperate zone, somewhere east of Eden.

We should have laughed out loud at the irony of it all. We really were east of Eden and closing in on it fast. We drove west from Port Angeles on highway 101 through Sappho and Beaver. Then the road turned south, skirting the foothills of Mount Olympus. Following the High River to the peninsula's western edge, we soon found ourselves at the gates of North America's garden of delight, the Queets rain forest. Angels with swords should have been there to keep the fallen away, but the narrow road was ours alone. Soon we found ourselves in the valley, surrounded by darkening green quiet.

There was a campground at the end of the road, and it was nearly empty. We selected a spot overlooking the Queets River, and I got out to guide Mark into the site.

At least that was the theory. I was supposed to stand at the back of the Phoenix and use hand signals he could see in a mirror to direct him into position without falling off a cliff or crushing something. What really happened was so stupid we were lucky no one was around to watch.

I climbed out of my seat and assumed a logical position at the back corner of the truck. I looked up to check for low-hanging tree branches. I looked down to check for low-lying impediments like logs or boulders or stray puppies. Then I started waving. "Come back, come back," I gestured. "Come back more." The Phoenix had about ten feet to cover, but it moved backwards about nine inches and stopped. I waved some more. The Phoenix didn't budge. The door on the driver's side opened. Mark climbed out. He lumbered toward me with daggers shooting from his eyes. "You're doing it all wrong," he shouted. "Hold your hands like this, and don't stand there. Stand here." If this sounds fairly civil, it's because I've purged the expletives.

I had a choice of two responses. I could blast him with a reciprocal salvo of contumely, or I could dispense an annoying whimper. Either one would draw further invective. I whimpered. He roared. Then he stormed back to the driver's seat.

I heard him throw the truck into reverse, and he backed up way too fast. Wham! The Phoenix smacked a tree stump. The impact put a noticeable dent into the back corner, and it cast an even darker pall over our spirits.

It was too late to go exploring, but too early to go to bed. Mark decided to build a fire, and I set up a folding chair in the moss on the riverbank. I wanted time to myself to sulk, and the darkening forest provided a perfect gloomy backdrop.

Thirty minutes later, there was still no fire, and Mark was in an even blacker mood than before. "I give up," he said finally. He went inside the Phoenix and slammed the door. I sat on the riverbank until darkness blotted out my surroundings. All was quiet except the river. All was serene except the battle raging in my soul.

We slept together in the bunk over the cab, and in our dreams we were lovers again. How can it be, I wondered, that we fight all day and then rest exhausted in one another's arms? Love burns and warms, rages and soothes, screams and whispers.

Sleep sponged up the day and delivered us a new morning. A luminous verdure glowed through the window, and I looked out into a primeval paradise. Moss-shrouded spruce trees reigned over a floor of ferns, and translucent maple leaves fluttered in the sunlight.

We walked through the forest in silence. The only sound came from our footsteps, and even those were muted by the soft carpet of leaves and lichen. The spruces and maples were completely shrouded in moss, great primeval festoons of it. A robust slug glistened on the path ahead of me, and great fungal shelves protruded from stumps and tree trunks. Everything was damp. Water glistened on the edges of leaves and dripped softly from the ferns.

A mile or so into the forest, a large spruce tree had fallen across the trail, and someone had sawed through it in two places to clear the path. The cuts looked fresh, the exposed wood almost pink against bark blackened by dampness. I touched the wood. It was wet, and it fell apart in my hand like canned tuna. "Who knows how long ago this was cut," I whispered to Mark. "This place lives under an eternal freshness spell."

Before my visit to Queets, I'd always thought of rain forests as tropical phenomena, places full of parrots and monkeys and huge constricting serpents. From my sojourn in Central America as a child, I also knew their denizens could be deadly, even the tiniest spider or most benign-looking caterpillar.

But the rain forests of the temperate zones are utterly different. Instead of palms and strangler figs, the northern pockets of heavy precipitation and mild temperature are home to conifers and maples. Instead of monkeys, you may find deer and bear and otter. The noisiest avian isn't a parrot, but a woodpecker. And if you're hoping for anacondas, forget it. The closest thing we came across was the slug.

All of which means that Queets pulses with a more muted vitality. It's a pregnant place, swelling with silent life and quiet activity. I was engulfed with the feeling that something supernatural was about to happen, that Merlin was peeking from behind a tree, that gnomes were watching from under mushrooms. There's magic in clear water and green stillness, and I soaked up the enchantment.

Somewhere along that soft trail, I lay my troubles down. Walking in that verdant Eden, I was innocent again, lost in the quiet wonder of a secluded paradise.

East Of The Cascades

Of course the baggage returned. I had yet to learn that you can't hire surroundings to do a human's job. Views can inspire you, sunsets can awe you, landscapes can challenge you, but not a one can transform you unless you cooperate. When all is said and done, you're the ferryman. You decide what stays in your boat and what turns into flotsam. It's not the river's job.

The river's task is to flow to the sea, and we followed it there, turning back towards Seattle when we reached the coast. We were headed east.

Everyone knows about East-West rivalries. The perennial clash between New York slick and LA slack caps the list, followed closely by classic sporting events like the Rose Bowl. What was new to me is the rift that runs through Washington and Oregon. It's a psychic fault line than runs north to south not far inland from the coast. To the west lie Seattle and Portland, home of global trend setters and backyard boat docks and rooms with a view. To the east lies, well, the east. It's the macaroni-and-cheese side of a poached salmon coastline.

Actually, that's putting it far too nicely. The inland zone is a region of dirty secrets, and because most of the area's population lives on the west side of the Cascades, the decisions to keep it that way keep on filtering down from above.

I mean, who's ever heard of the Tri-Cities? Sorry, Richland-Pasco-Kennewick, but you weren't part of my vocabulary until I saw your sign on Interstate 82. Oh, I suppose "Hanford Nuclear Reservation" rang a faint bell. Wasn't that where they built atom bombs during World War II?

When the Cold War thawed, the big new enterprise was nuclear power. The Columbia River could be harnessed once again to provide cooling, and who cared if the whole operation looked like an ugly scar and produced radioactive sewage? There was nobody important out there to notice.

For decades, the trend setters have been able to ignore their backyard, but times are changing. Nuclear waste doesn't just disappear. Giant underground tanks have kept it out of sight, but it won't be out of mind much longer. Tanks have a penchant for leaking, and toxic effluent with a half-life longer than *War and Peace* is slowly making its way into the aquifer. From there it will make its noxious way into the Columbia River. The Columbia River will bear it all to Portland, where coastal water patterns will soon share it with Seattle.

So what was I saying about jettisoning psychic baggage? It can still come back to haunt you, even if you dump it in the river. Simple ditching is only a temporary solution. For permanent results, you've got to change the stuff that bites you into something you can pet. Once transformed, it will either fly away on its own, or you won't mind having it around after all.

Clean isn't enough if a polluted river is the price. Unburdened isn't sufficient if true freedom is your goal. But what mystery turns lethal effluent into the water of life? By what baptism is a life transformed? With a sigh that stretched to the horizon, I realized that freedom doesn't arrive simply because your baggage is out of sight. Freedom knows you may have hidden it on the other side of the mountains. Freedom has the sneaking suspicion you may have dumped it into the river. Freedom stays just ahead of you, just out of your reach, a perennial horizon. It's there waiting at the vanishing point, that ever receding destination that can only be achieved when you quit faking, when you've cleaned up your act so well that a god will drink the wash water.

I sighed again, disgusted with my own sophistry, my own spineless words that had no agenda to give them a skeleton. It's easy to spew platitudes and wax eloquent, but the universe expands on action. I had no idea how to solve the problem of nuclear waste. I couldn't even get along with my husband. I was a fine one to be pontificating about major environmental issues in the Pacific Northwest.

And the eastern sides of Washington and Oregon are not wastelands. They hold some of the most fascinating, beautiful and pristine places in the country. The best apples in the world hail from orchards around Yakima, and on toward Spokane, there's the glory of the Selkirk Mountains. Walla Walla is more than just a jolly name. The Oregon Trail ended in the Willamette Valley, where homesteading pioneers found a rainbow's end in the green hills and rolling river.

Wisdom Comes To Us In Dreams

We stopped in Pendleton after we crossed the Oregon border, a town that revels in the afterglow of its wild west heyday. Its famous woolen mills turn out thousands of yards of distinctive plaid fabric and Indian-inspired blankets every day, and welcome the public to don ear protectors and walk through the whole clattering operation.

We camped by the river, where a young entrepreneur named Rick was trolling for tourists. He said he was a third-generation resident of Pendleton, and he offered an insider's tour of the surrounding countryside. We were his only charges that warm afternoon.

"First we'll go through the Umatilla Indian Reservation," he said as we climbed into his van. Driving east from town, he pointed out the tribal headquarters and told us a casino was about to open on reservation land. "Every Indian who wants a job is guaranteed one," he said, "But the interesting thing is, many of them don't want jobs, so what will probably happen is the same thing that's happened with their farmland. Much of it is worked by white tenant farmers.

"Most outsiders think this means that Indians just want to live off government handouts, but it's not true. What we're seeing is what's always happened when two totally different cultures are thrown together. Whites think that if Indians don't want nine-to-five jobs, it has to be because they're lazy. To the Umatillas, nine-to-five jobs are a foreign weirdness. They've always been a migratory nation, moving according to the seasons, living off the land.

"The Umatillas aren't farmers, never have been. So when the government gave them the ownership of land, which, by the way, was also an alien concept, most of them didn't have the slightest inclination to work it. In fact, it flew in the face of everything they held sacred. The result was that they rented it out to people who wanted to farm. In some cases, they sold their parcels.

"The casino is a similar situation. I won't be surprised if very few Indians end up working there. Even though times are changing, it's still not their custom to 'hold jobs' in the way white folks do.

"The Umatillas used to be famous horse breeders, and horses were an important part of their lifestyle. They gave them mobility, an essential for nomadic people. See that house there? It's very modest, but the truck parked next to it is nice and new. That says it all. They're movers, not sitters. They like to be on the road."

Houses and farms stretched out in all directions. Just as Rick said, it was easy to tell which farms were being operated by tenants. They were Norman Rockwell classic, with neat farmhouses, barns, windmills. The Indian establishments were ramshackle, with abandoned furniture dotting the yards and old cars serving as chicken coops. Barefoot children played in the dust. Good old European feudalism had been set on its head. These were the manor houses.

With a 200-year history of failed communication, mutual mistrust, and gross inequity of power, it's remarkable that Native American culture has survived at all. As recently as 1877, after newly developed agricultural methods made the Umatillas' reservation a potential farming gold mine, the editor of Pendleton's East Oregonian newspaper wrote, "We favor their removal, for it is a burning shame to keep this fine body of land for a few worthless Indians."

The U.S. government shared the view. Not far from Pendleton lies the fertile Wallowa Valley, the homeland of the Nez Percé nation. Eighteen seventy-seven was the year the U.S. Army received orders to remove the Nez Percé so that white settlers could turn the land into farms. The resulting conflict ended only after Chief Joseph led 600 warriors, women, children and old men on one of the longest and most acclaimed retreats in military history. After three months and more than a thousand miles, the cavalry caught the Nez Percé forty miles shy of the Canadian Border. Chief Joseph and his people, starving and freezing in an early winter, were shipped off to Oklahoma. "I will fight no more forever," said Chief Joseph when he surrendered.

The same Chief had once authored these words: "The Earth was created by the assistance of the sun, and it should be left as it was. The country was made without lines of demarcation, and it is no man's business to divide it." How can such a leader find common ground with the sons of Cincinnatus, men who had been marking lines on land since Adam's fall?

"My young men shall never work," wrote another leader, the Wanapum shaman Smohalla. "Men who work cannot dream; and wisdom comes to us in dreams. You ask me to plow the ground. Shall I take a knife and tear my mother's breast? .You ask me to cut grass and make hay and sell it and be rich like white men. But how dare I cut off my mother's hair?"

I'm sorry, but if you say "I won't work" to us creatures of Judeo-Christian heritage, it's the same as saying "I'm shiftless." And if you admit to teaching your children lazy ways, well God damn you. It gives us, who have the proof of might to justify the truth of our philosophy, the divine obligation to do our best to straighten you out. And if we can't get you to see how terrific our kind of work is, or at least how wonderful it is to establish fiefdoms and build fences, well, we'll just have to pick you up and dump you in a nasty place with no water and no cable television. In other words, if we can't exploit you or your land profitably, then we'll exile you.

This line of thinking is the reason that Native Americans own most of Palm Springs, California, real estate that ranks with the most valuable in the country. Who could have guessed, a century ago, that a barren stretch of desert would become as trendy as Fifth Avenue? Indians in Arizona are having an ultimate laugh next door to Scottsdale, where their once valueless reservation is juxtaposed to some of the city's most exclusive residential developments.

And then there's the casino phenomenon, that started with bingo parlors sixty miles east of Los Angeles, and recently culminated in an enormous gambling hall even closer than that to New York City. What was I saying about trying to ditch things you want to lose in secret places? Well, it doesn't work with people any better than it does with nuclear waste. Hidden wrongs are cancers, quiet murderers that extinguish peace as utterly as open war.

Peace can be as elusive as freedom, I thought. If it can't sprout in a single breast, it can never sweep the land. As we drove east once more, I knew my challenge was to find harmony within. I had to find a way "to fight no more forever."

·9·

A Sharp Stick In The Eye

Standing On The Plexiglass Elevator

I dreamed I looked down and found I wasn't standing on anything. Below me was an abyss, a rock chasm with tiny white rapids crashing at the bottom. Suddenly a hand touched my shoulder. I turned to find a being—an angel?—standing beside me. He was smiling. "You haven't noticed," he said, "But you're standing on a plexiglass elevator. That's why you haven't fallen."

I looked at my feet. They were indeed supported by something hard, even if it was invisible. I knelt down and rapped the surface with my knuckles. The being seemed to be right. We were standing on a transparent platform.

"I hate heights, " I said.

The being laughed. "I followed you out here, you know. You're the one who climbed up to the edge of the canyon and stepped off."

"I did?" I asked incredulously. "You didn't bring me here?"

"I followed you here, sweetheart," he said. "I thought you might panic when you looked down. I thought you might not notice the elevator."

And then he was gone. I stood on my invisible pedestal for what seemed like an eternity, afraid to move, afraid to break the spell. The air was cool and still, and if I listened carefully, I could just hear the sound of the river far below.

Suddenly an eagle flew past my head, and I awoke. Idaho was outside my window.

Telephones From The Future

Northern Idaho is like a store-bought cheesecake. It spends most of its life frozen, but when it thaws out, it's so delicious you want to eat the whole thing at one sitting. It's the same way Californians in the 1980's felt about Sandpoint and Coeur d'Alene and Sagle and Koetenai. They were sick of smog and traffic and commutes, and they could sell their houses for sums no one else in the country could believe. One ordinary split-level in a Los Angeles suburb could be swapped for a dream house and fifty acres on Lake Pend Oreille. Many of them failed to realize they were getting seven months of arctic winter thrown in for free.

We stayed at a small, oversubscribed campground in Coeur d'Alene. Driven by a desire to shoehorn as many tents, trailers, cars and campers into two acres as he could, the owner had split and re-split all his electrical connections. Black cords were draped over tree branches and dangled from telephone poles, a snarled black licorice web. We should have known better, but we plugged ourselves in. Meltdown occurred immediately, and our super-strength surge protector exploded in a puff of smoke. When I tried to make a telephone call, we discovered that our cellular system had been lobotomized by the same jolt. I suppose I should have been grateful that nothing else met its end, but I was an hour away from a deadline, and I wasn't in a mood to be looking for silver linings.

And here's why I'll always have a soft spot for Coeur d'Alene. We drove into town to look for a fax machine or some other device by which I might achieve data transfer. The most imposing building was the tall resort hotel right on the edge of the lake. "Maybe they have a 'business center'" said Mark. "And even if they don't, we could have a drink in the bar." Escapist it might have been, but it struck my fancy perfectly.

But we never made it to the bar. In the lobby, someone whose boots I'd like to kiss had installed telephones at a marble counter top overlooking the lake. You could sit in a comfortable chair and call anyone you wanted using a credit card. That alone would have been pleasant, but my mood soared when I discovered that these phones had been shipped to Idaho from the future. They had data jacks on the side.

I did not walk. I ran back to the Phoenix and packed up my laptop. One more time, I'd found a wormhole to cyberspace. One more time, I'd filed my story the good new-fashioned way.

As marvelous as the phones at the Coeur d'Alene resort were, they couldn't erase the fact that our cellular system was now useless. It took four weeks, hundreds of dollars, and a very nice man in Spokane to get it working again.

"No Mortgage, No Gardener—You Must Save A Lot Of Money"

Which brings me to another topic that never seems to go away. Wherever we roam, in the flesh or online, we never cover very much ground before we hear someone saying, "It must be great to be able to live so inexpensively. No mortgage, no gardener—you must save a lot of money."

Well, here's the truth of the matter. It's a fact that if you have only a shoestring, it might stretch farther if you live in a trailer than just about any other style of housing. I mean, what are your choices? A cramped apartment? A motel that charges by the week? It's not hard to find a trailer for practically nothing, and trailer parks are generally nicer places for kids and dogs than apartment houses. You might even be able to plant a garden.

Please note, however, that the one thing the trailer home does not provide is mobility. Shoestrings don't stretch far enough to buy tires and gas and overnight camping spots. If saving money is your object, the wheels won't turn.

In 1998, you could rent a spot in a decent trailer park for $150 a month. The same establishment charged $28 a night for those who wanted to stay just a day or two. That adds up to $840 a month, which is a pretty hefty markup.

If you stayed in one place, you could get telephone service for as little as $8 a month. Between long distance calls on pay phones and our cellular bill, we shelled out as much as $850, and that was before we started publishing a web site. For a year, our cell bill never fell below $1500 a month.

Oh, but surely you're unusual, I hear you say. Most people wouldn't be so fanatically wedded to the notion of mobile communication. Well, it's true. Most people aren't. But most people are mobile only when they're "on vacation," or "on a trip." It's temporary. To see whether we truly qualify as fanatics, ask them to do without their home telephone for a month, and while you're at it, take away their cable television and daily mail service.

Speaking of mail, it's something else that's usually free to the receiver if you stay in one spot. That changes when you're all over the map. We had a shipping address in California. All our mail went to a company that held on to it until we told them via long distance telephone call where to send it. They packed it up, affixed new postage, and sent it off to catch us. If we were moving fast enough, they'd have to send it "overnight." Everything included, it cost us about $50 to get a week's worth of mail. Sometimes it was more, if we were lucky enough to pay overnight shipping charges on a California telephone book or a fat mail order catalog. And sometimes it missed us, and we'd have to cough up the dough to do it all over again. And sometimes we'd get somebody else's mail.

The vast disparity between living on a roll and "living in a trailer" makes for fascinating juxtapositions in campgrounds. In a city, the rich folks are cordoned off from the poor ones by carefully maintained lines of demarcation. You don't find a shanty next door to a chateau. But in a trailer park, you can! A rolling Versailles might be parked right next to a decrepit camper with rotting tires. You can find the richest people in America parked cheek-by-jowl with the ones who have the least. You can peek over the dashboard and watch the Vanderbilts dine on bone china while watching a big screen TV. Ten feet away, Ma Kettle, Pa Kettle, and five little Kettles are outside eating beanie weenie out of a can.

We were Vanderbilts on a Kettle budget. Our vehicle looked like something a movie star might drive, but we had no idea how we'd pay our next phone bill. Our income was practically nonexistent, but nobody looking at us would have guessed.

Because we weren't poor. We were too overprivileged to qualify, even when our pockets were empty. We were rich, even though we ate beanie weenie and wore socks with holes in them.

All of which makes me wonder. Were we rich, and pretending to be poor? Or were we poor pretending we were rich? Are appearances deceiving, or are they dead giveaways?

Once, when we were lost in a maze of narrow streets in Alexandria, Virginia, two men in worn jackets and dirty trousers approached us. It was a cold night, and the temperature was dropping. The men had pulled their collars up around their ears. "We need money to stay in a hotel," the taller one said. We had just been wondering the usual, how to buy gas, how to get food. Mark said, "We don't have any cash." It was true.

"I have to go to a money machine," Mark continued. "Maybe then I can help you." We drove on, and two blocks away, we saw a bank on a corner. An automatic teller machine glowed near the door, and, miraculously, there was room to park right next to it. Mark got out and extracted forty dollars, which brought our balance alarmingly close to zero.

We drove on, moving circuitously through the narrow old streets. We had no idea how to find the two men again, and we weren't entirely sure we wanted to. Then, suddenly, blocks and blocks from where we'd first met them, they materialized in front of us. They smiled and ran up to Mark's window, greeting him like an old friend.

"We knew you'd come back," said the taller one. Mark reached into his pocket and pulled out a twenty-dollar bill. "Thank you," said the man. "Now we can stay in a nice hotel."

"God bless you," called the other, and they sprinted away. We found a highway, drove south, and, after seeking the indulgence of the night guard, spent the night in a Wal-Mart parking lot.

I'm Nobody. Who Are You?

The day after the fire, when I was technically homeless, I remember driving to a supermarket to buy a toothbrush and shampoo. As I left the store, a man wearing a filthy pea coat and pushing a shopping cart stuffed with plastic bags and old blankets asked me if I had any change. "I'm homeless," he said unnecessarily.

I gave him my change, thinking all the while, "You'd probably be surprised to know that I am, too." But I wasn't. Houseless, maybe, but homeless, no. There's a difference, and it has nothing to do with physical reality.

Even though our business burned, we were somehow never "unemployed." After the fire, I read in the newspaper that self-employed people who were wiped out could get unemployment benefits. I showed the story to Mark, and he went to the unemployment office to find out how it all worked.

He returned within an hour. "I couldn't do it," he said. "I walked in the door and took one look at that sad line and the burnt-out people behind the counter. 'I can't be unemployed,' I said to myself. 'I'm sorry, but I'm just not cut out for it.'" Just as I had found I wasn't homeless, Mark had discovered he wasn't unemployed.

We act like unemployment and homelessness are absolutes, that they're appropriately descriptive of situations beyond an individual's control. They aren't. They're just words, as formless as any other abstraction. They float harmlessly in the ether until someone screens them onto t-shirts. People see them, and they say, "Hey, that's me," or "Hey, that's Joe." Emblazoned on a chest, they become labels. Plucked out of the world of ideas and given three dimensions, they wield the power of concrete immutability. They start looking like truth. They start defining personality. They are the emperor's new clothes, mass produced for all takers. They are the most expensive raiment in the world, even though they're often proffered with a handout. Their price is freedom, and while you're busy exchanging it for a mess of pottage, it seems only fair to throw your pride in too.

"It's easy for you to say," you may well reply. "You've never been truly hungry or truly poor. You've got an ivy-covered education and skin as white as snow. What can you possibly know about real lack? My god, you drive around in a truck built for a Arab prince. You're leading the life the rest of us are scrounging toward and may never achieve. Who the hell are you to talk about the price of freedom?"

"I'm nobody," says my Emily Dickinson side. "Who are you?"

Who are you, really and truly? People everywhere wear the labels that give them what they need and identify the role they play in the world. They wear "homeless," and "jobless" and "rich" and "privileged." They wear "mother" and "brother," and "cop" and "robber." But no matter how plastered over in epithets a body becomes, somewhere underneath the shell there's a winged victory, a free spirit that bears no onus of label, no weight of lack. It knows no hunger, needs no clothes and wallows not in ephemeral quagmires.

It's a nobody, because it can't be taxed or jailed or scared. It's invisible until that fateful moment when it thrusts a sharp stick in the eye of apparent reality. "Nobody's hurting me!" the Cyclops cries. Nobody. That invisible being, that free spirit, that magic self that defies gravity. It's me. It's you. We're standing on a plexiglass elevator, looking at a river crashing miles below.

· 10 ·

Eastern Winter, Western Thaw

Separate Snowdrifts

Whether you're in Texas or Tennessee, if you ask someone the best time to visit, they always say October. Since I can't have twelve Octobers in a row, I'm loathe to squander one when it rolls around. Have you seen the Smoky Mountains as fall steals over their ridges and valleys? Have you watched the autumnal sun slide down over the gardens of Monticello, the Craters of the Moon, the Golden Gate? October's a golden month, summer's payoff.

That first year on the road, October surrounded us with a canopy of glory, but I hardly noticed. Looking back, I have to tell myself that the Midwest clothes itself in brilliance before winter sets in. I can barely remember the whirls of autumn leaves born on breezes over golden fields. I was blinded by self-absorption. I wallowed in private desolation no exterior paradise could penetrate. I skipped over fall and withdrew into a winter of discontent.

As much as I had hoped to find peace inside myself and in my relationship with Mark, it still eluded me. Was I feeling the vacuum left behind by the fire? Was stuff important after all? Did I miss the solid ordinariness of my commuting days, the predictable comfort of a house on a hill, a car in a garage, the six o'clock news? Could it be possible I wasn't meant to be a wanderer after all? "No, no, no!" I screamed in silence. "It's not that at all. I don't want it back. I don't. I didn't miss it when I first saw the black gap, and I don't miss it now."

If not that, then what? It was a question whose answer was as inscrutable as Mark's dark silence. We were strangers, he and I, lost in a foreign zone of unexpected conflict. Mark wanted to spend the winter in Wyoming. I couldn't understand why. Why shovel snow if your house has wheels?

"I want to see if I can do it," he said.

"I don't," I replied. And that was one of our friendlier interchanges.

Before the first hibernal flurry, we parted. I caught a plane to the east coast, climbing aboard with little notion of what I might do or where I might stay. I passed a frigid winter in Montreal and New York, proving, if nothing else, that weather wasn't what dragged Mark and me into separate snow drifts.

What sucked us into a winter of despair? At the time I was snowblind, unable to see through the opaque storm that raged in my soul. Looking back, though, it's as clear as a blue sky after a blizzard. We'd planned and schemed, but mostly we'd just dealt with superficial issues, like where we'd go and what we'd see. We thought we'd done a good job of choosing a new path, of reinventing our lives, but we'd ignored the invisible tie that bound us.

We'd taken our relationship for granted. It was fireproof, after all, like all truly important stuff. Love exists on another plane, impervious to mundane disaster. It was supposed to conquer all, wasn't it? If it was as wonderful as it was supposed to be, surely it didn't need tending and weeding. Shouldn't it just flourish on its own?

Maybe the answer should have been obvious, but it took a season in the deep freeze before a new light glimmered. If our lives were to blossom afresh, our marriage needed at least as much attention as our wheels. We had to look at it as willingly as we'd looked at the black gap, and it was up to us to decide how to redefine our partnership.

Even while we were apart, we stayed in touch by e-mail and telephone. Looking back, I realize that while Mark was facing ice storms in the west, while I sipped espresso in the east, we were still together in that invisible place where moth, rust and fire can't go. Love conquered after all. At the end of January, I met Mark in Denver.

Home Is Where Your Dog Is

Mark and I were happy to see each other, but Marvin was nothing less than ecstatic to find the three of us reunited. Even two days later, he jumped into my lap every time I sat down. He was a little large to be a lapdog, but it didn't matter. If he'd been a Great Dane, he would have been welcome to knock me down. I was in a mood for unbridled displays of affection, and Marvin was determined to provide them.

Marvin was a stray puppy when we first met him. A friend had discovered him howling near his door. Manny had tried to find his owners, but a month of searching had produced no results. The day he set out to take the puppy to the pound, he stopped by our house on the way.

"I just thought I'd show him to you," Manny said to Mark. "I have to get rid of him before my kids get any more attached to him." Manny never got to the pound that day, and that's how Marvin embarked on a life that eventually turned him into a road dog.

"Marvin had a great adventure while you were gone," said Mark. "He touched noses with a cow."

I'd been with Marvin the day he first visited a beach, got chased by waves, tasted salt water. I often wondered what went on inside his shaggy head, what he really thought, what he really knew. He was even more inscrutable than Mark.

"I had an adventure with a cow, too," Mark went on. "A mean one tried to gore me, and she came close to succeeding."

"You should've touched noses first," I said. "We could both learn lessons from Marvin."

And the fact is, Marvin has taught us a lot. When he's frightened by thunder, I comfort him and remember that I, too, waste energy fearing things that are better ignored. When he approaches other dogs with alacrity, I find myself following his example and greeting their owners with a smile. And Marvin knows the true meaning of home. It has nothing to do with house or address or even bed. Home is where the people who love you are, and even when he was an abandoned puppy, Marvin knew how to find one.

Rocky Mountain Catacomb

Denver is such a surprise. You expect the alpine meadows and bubbling streams and snow-capped peaks of beer advertisements and John Denver songs, but what you really get is a flat arid plain. Even though it wasn't even February yet, there wasn't any snow on the ground when I arrived. The air was so warm that most of the natives were wearing shorts. We headed west on Interstate 40, and drove until we caught sight of a sign that said "Indian Springs."

"Hot springs!" exclaimed Mark. "Let's stop." I wasn't about to argue. Hot springs are proof that God exists, that bathing antedates civilization, that luxury can be a naturally occurring phenomenon. Having just arrived from the gelid East, I thrilled to the thought of sliding into a steaming cauldron under a Rocky Mountain moon. Mark took the next exit off the highway, and we followed signs through the small town of Idaho Springs and up a hill.

The sun was just beginning to fall behind the mountains as we climbed the wooden steps of the old hotel. Warm lights glowed from every window, and an amiable clerk gave us a list of services and told us where we could park the Phoenix. As we stood at the desk, a door opened and out stepped a man and a woman, wrinkled and pink. Little wisps of steam still rose from their hair. It was then we realized that the hotel was built not near the springs, but right over them.

Beneath our feet were two gender-segregated, clothing-optional "caves" carved into the bedrock, and several "private baths," concrete-walled rooms equipped with large square plastered tubs. We signed up for an hour in one of the latter. In the meantime, we strolled down the hallways of the old hotel looking at pictures of Sarah Bernhardt, Jesse James, and the other notables who'd soaked their bones here.

Geothermic activity draws humans the way candles attract moths, and people have been hovering around Indian Springs since a prospector named George Jackson noticed the creek was hot in 1859. The resort was built ten years later, after Idaho Springs had enjoyed a growth spurt begun by George's other discovery, a good-sized gold nugget. The buildings we were walking through were first erected in 1905, and they'd been expanding ever since.

After we parked the Phoenix, we returned for our appointed hour of bathing. The desk clerk handed us towels and, picking up a large jailer's key ring, led us to the door downstairs. We descended in a cloud of sulphurous steam, feeling like two new denizens of the underworld. At the end of a dank hall, our guide unlocked a narrow door. Inside, water dripped steadily into the pool from the low ceiling, and the walls were crusted with a century of mineral deposits. The cubicle was dimly lit by a single naked bulb.

"Here you go," said Mephistopheles. "If you need anything, I'm upstairs." He departed, leaving us to our private catacomb. I didn't get my Rocky Mountain moon, but hot water is great under any circumstances, and even better when you don't have to wear a bathing suit.

All's Right with the World

Is there another geologic phenomenon that has inspired such a variety of social and spiritual practice among humans than hot springs? Volcanos may have rivaled them in an earlier age, but hot springs are timeless in their ability to cause people of all persuasions to invent customs and practice ritual.

Hot springs improved by the hand of man offer an appealing menu of indulgences, but the best place for taking the waters is in the wild, in naturally heated water undisciplined by civilization. My favorite hot springs boast no rules, no mores, and no clothes. And where's the best hot spring? Is it on the Rio Grande in Big Bend country or on a mountaintop in the Canadian Rockies? High in Montana's Bitterroots, or in a palm grove in the California desert? Yes, yes, yes, but only under one simple circumstance. The best hot spring is the one you are floating in, half-submerged under a full moon.

And if the moon is invisible because you are fifty feet underground in a lime-encrusted chamber, all's still right with the world. All was right with our world, anyway. Mark and I slipped into the healing water, and as it warmed our bodies, it thawed our hearts. The road stretched ahead of us, and we were fellow adventurers once more.

· 11 ·

A Perfect Juncture
Of Time And Space

On The Road Again

It's exceedingly easy to laugh at country music, to sneer at a hayseed drawl and an admonishment to stand by your man. It's so unsophisticated, so hillbilly, so twangy. Of all the music in the world, it's the most incapable of being dressed in the emperor's new clothes. Country music greets its audience unabashedly naked, free of complex harmonies, minor keys, leit motifs.

It's the music of trucks and dogs and too much booze, of broken hearts and extra aces. It's the music of Muskogee, Chattanooga and Fort Worth, broadcasted from Branson and Nashville and New York City.

Yes, New York. If Garth Brooks can draw a mob in Central Park, it's proof indisputable that if Walt Whitman heard America singing in the nineties, the song would be "On the Road Again."

And so it was that Kenny Rogers sang us south, and Willie Nelson got us all the way to Four Corners.

Four Corners would be nowhere at all if white folks hadn't drawn two intersecting lines on a map over a century ago. That simple act turned a flat, dry plain into a tourist attraction, a place where we, like thousands of other visitors every year, paid two dollars to bend over and put one hand in Colorado, one hand in Utah, and a foot each in Arizona and New Mexico. The Navajo nation pockets the money, a charming irony. The Navajo care not a whit about state lines, but the marker happens to lie on their land.

South of Albuquerque is a town called Socorro, which is short for El Pueblo de Nuestra Señora del Socorro, the Village of Our Lady of Succor. Called Pilabó by its earlier residents, the settlement's new name was bestowed in 1598 by members of the exploring cadre of Juan de Oñate. The town had appeared just when they needed it.

Migrating birds may well feel the same way about the place. The valley of the Rio Grande lies under the flyway of the avian nations that follow the call of the seasons. Every year a myriad of sandhill cranes, Arctic geese, and a wide variety of ducks wing their way south from the Yukon, the Northwest Territories, Hudson Bay. Like Juan de Oñate and his cohorts, they stop at Socorro for sustenance.

Actually they put down a little to the south, at a place called Bosque del Apache. It's a National Wildlife Preserve, where the natural food and water supplies get a little help from the hand of man. The U.S. Fish and Wildlife Service manages a network of dikes and canals, ensuring that when the birds arrive, the preserve will be able to support them.

The first white wave of birds is always greeted by a host of ornithophiles, heavily-equipped photographers, enthusiastic reporters, and scores of tourists. And then, as the birds settle into their daily routine, the people wander off. By February, which is when we appeared on the scene, we were among only a handful of two-legged interlopers.

"You have to get up before dawn," Dee Brown had said. Dee, who lives in Albuquerque, is the person who'd told us about the Bosque, and admonished us not to miss it. "Drive into the preserve while it's still dark, and park on one of the dikes, in between the marshes, where the birds spend the night, and the open fields, where they go to feed during the day. Then just sit there. Watch the sun come up. Watch what happens."

We drove into the Bosque before four. No moon broke the darkness. We parked in a wide place on a dirt embankment, and turned out the lights. They seemed like a harsh intrusion in the stillness. I made coffee in the dark, and we sipped it silently. A warm breeze blew, and the leaves of a cottonwood brushed the roof of the Phoenix. Otherwise, all was quiet.

Softly, slowly, the sky lightened. Mingling with the gray, a pink tinge gradually stole over the horizon. We stepped outside to watch and feel the dry breeze against our faces. The sky turned orange as the sun broke the horizon, and, was it my imagination? I could swear a sound accompanied the sun's arrival. Was it a collective coo, or the rustle of a thousand wings? It was gone on the breeze as quickly as it came to my ears, and the sun rose higher, spreading a blanket of purple and pink and orange over the landscape.

And then it wasn't my imagination any more. Secret avian conversations rose from the marsh as its denizens greeted the day. Suddenly, without warning, a great white phalanx of wings burst over the trees. As the birds rose higher, they turned black against the sun and surged towards us.

The sound started as a quiet rush and quickly rose to a great flapping roar, its percussive rhythm encompassing us as we fumbled with our cameras. I snapped a few pictures and then gave up. A few blurred snapshots couldn't begin to capture the sound, the wind, the raw beauty of a thousand birds soaring as one. I stood there, trying to soak up enough to last me the rest of my life.

I couldn't, of course, but not for lack of trying. We stayed until the last duck had flown quacking to the feeding grounds and the sun was halfway overhead. We came back for the evening retreat, and we came back the next morning to watch the marshes awaken one more time before heading north.

I still think of those beating wings and the call of the cranes. Whenever my world collapses, whenever I withdraw into an ever-shrinking universe of self-absorption, I remember that there are galaxies not so far away, vast storms of wings riding on highways I'll never know. They rise on the wind and beat their way to the ends of the earth. They don't know me. They don't care. And somehow, when I think of them, my cares vanish, too, on a great white phalanx of rushing wings.

Angel Fire

We drove north, following license plates that read "Land of Enchantment." After the birds, I was beginning to think New Mexico wasn't boasting, but just making an obvious comment. And I'd been thinking, ever since we first set wheel to road, that someday, somewhere, we'd probably want to stop, to—for desperate lack of a better word—settle. Why is it that when people set out on journeys, they immediately start thinking about their ends? We laugh at children who ask "Are we there yet?" But secretly we never stop asking the same thing ourselves.

I thought New Mexico might be my destination, the place that would say to me, "You're home, sweetheart! Take your shoes off!" I was hoping, in fact. It seemed like we'd been traveling long enough. Hadn't we said six months or a year?

Taos is a name of romance, of art, of gritty history. Kit Carson lived there, and scores of writers and artists. Might not some fanciful adobe call our names as we walked past? I thought all this, and hoped all this, as we drove up the mountainside and onto the high plain.

We parked in a dusty lot on the edge of town. A man was breaking wild ponies in the next field. We walked through the business district, looking in window after window of paintings and weavings and baskets and sculpture. We went inside Kit Carson's house, and toured the erstwhile home of the painter Ernest Blumenschein. We had espresso in a coffee house founded by psychotherapists who'd emigrated from California.

It was obvious from the moment we stepped inside the door that Elizabeth and Richard had become fixtures in their community. They greeted everyone except us by name, and when we left, we knew we'd be remembered if we came back. The Taos Coffee Company was a village in itself. Elizabeth and Richard had created a home. I envied them. I want a home, too, I thought.

As we walked the streets of Taos, I longed for it to feel like something more. But it didn't. It was just beautiful and dusty and not mine. With a sigh and one last cappuccino from the Taos Coffee Company, we drove north again, high into a valley surrounded by the Sangre de Cristo range.

Named for the blood of Christ, these mountains have a forbidding harshness about them. In a good winter, they soften
under some of the best snow in the world, but in dry times, they
stand sharp and bare all year, and the people suffer. They need
a heavy influx of skiers every year to survive.

The nearer slopes were bare as we drew near Eagle Nest,
and the sun was getting ready to slide down behind the range to
the west. It was windy and cold, and we had the road to ourselves. As I surveyed the landscape, I caught sight of what looked
like a white sail rising from a nearby ridge. "What is that thing?"
I asked Mark, but it was already behind us.

We drove to a small campground on the edge of Eagle Nest
Lake, which, being frozen, was almost indistinguishable from
dry land. As we drove off the road, we sank into gravelly slush
and snow, and Mark shifted into four-wheel drive to get across
the parking lot. In spite of the hostile weather, the campground
was open for business, and a pleasant man greeted us inside the
office. "Do you sell propane?" asked Mark as we registered.
"We're nearly out." The Phoenix One has high clearance, but the
price is a tiny propane tank. The furnace can suck it dry in one
day if the weather demands that we run it nonstop.

"No, I don't, but you'll need your furnace tonight," the man
said. "There's a place down the road. Hold on, though, because
it's close to quittin' time. Let me call and make sure they'll wait
for you."

Soon we were headed back down the road we'd just traveled. Again the white sail on the hillside caught my eye. This
time Mark saw it, too. "What is that thing?" we cried in unison.
It vanished behind us. We arrived at the propane place after it
had officially closed, but thanks to our intercessor's telephone
call, someone was waiting to fill up our tank. He was swathed in
a large muffler, and he pointed to a thermometer hanging on the
wall of the office. "27 and falling," he said over the wind. "It's
gonna be a brisk one."

For the third time, we passed the white sail. This time,
Mark slowed down, and, looking carefully, we saw that a road
wound down from the hillside to meet the one we were on, and
at the intersection, there was a sign. D.A.V. Viet Nam Memorial,
it read.

"Let's go up there tomorrow," I said, and Mark agreed. "It's called to us three times," he said. "That means we have to answer."

The morning dawned cold and clear, and we headed straight for the little road up to the sail. At the top of the hill we found an empty parking lot and a low edifice. A few hundred feet away was the sail. "It's a building," I said, but the wind whipped my words away over the valley.

The structure in front of us seemed deserted, but when we neared the door, a woman appeared. "Come on in," she said. "We're working on the floor in here, but if you don't mind the mess, you're more than welcome." We stepped inside, and as our eyes adjusted to the interior dimness, we skirted the mop buckets and saw that we were in a sort of museum.

Large photographs hung on the walls. They were images of Viet Nam, of soldiers and children and girls in pretty dresses, of guns and mines and hand grenades. Suddenly, unexpectedly, I was drawn back into the war that never really ended, that still sears wounds into the souls of those who served.

It was never my own conflict. I wasn't draftable, nor did I have a friend, a father, a brother, a lover who was. No one close to me perished, and those veterans I did know spoke little. It was a newspaper story to me, a catalyst for campus unrest, a political stance. It was distant, impersonal, somebody else's war.

The photographs in that room changed all that. In that quiet space, surrounded by images of intensity, of fatigue-clad youths laughing and staring and dying, I could no longer distance myself. Viet Nam was no longer thousands of miles away. It was here in the mountains named for the blood of Christ. It was now.

The place was a visitors' center for the sail, and the sail, we learned, was a chapel built by Victor Westphall. He started working on the project five days after his son David, a Marine infantry officer, was killed in Viet Nam in 1968.

After we looked at the pictures, we turned up our collars and faced the wind again. We followed a path down a slope to the chapel, which was small and round. Inside, narrow windows framed views of the mountains, and a photograph of David Westphall hung on one wall.

We weren't alone. A man was sitting on one of the stone tiers that form benches facing the center of the sanctuary. We sat down next to him. As I turned to look, I saw a tear steal down his cheek. It was matched by a tear on my own, and when I looked at Mark, his eyes were glistening, too. And so we sat in silence, listening to the wind, letting it wail for the fallen, letting it howl for the pain of those who returned.

I can't tell you what transcendent spirit lives at Angel Fire, and no one could tell us how the place got such a haunting name. I can't tell you why being there evoked not only sorrow and despair, but also healing and hope. I can't tell you why, as I write these words, tears again fill my eyes. It's as though the absolute worst and best of humanity is distilled there, waiting to bestow comfort and light on those who are willing to embrace the shadow.

When we came down from the mountain, we returned to the campground by the frozen lake. When we drove in, we were greeted by a man wearing a hat adorned with an embroidered patch that identified him as a Viet Nam veteran. "I'm Tom," he said. "I heard about your truck, and I was hoping you'd be back so I could see it." After answering his questions about the Phoenix, Mark said, "We were just visiting the Angel Fire memorial. It's quite a place."

"It is, isn't it?" said Tom. "I discovered this valley by accident when I was driving across country three years ago. I lived in Pennsylvania, and I wasn't really thinking about moving, but when I came over the hill, I suddenly had this overwhelming feeling that I was home. It didn't go away, so I brought my family back to visit. They all decided, even my teen-age daughter, that they wanted to move here. As we settled in, I found out about the memorial, and I discovered that I wasn't the only veteran who had felt the call of the place. There are lots of us here. I can't explain it. It's almost spooky."

As we walked around the lake that evening, I looked out over the valley, and once again up at the mountains. I was hoping I'd hear the same call Tom had, but the mountains were stern and silent, and the lake lay frozen and still. Even the wind had died to a whisper, and no comforting voice emerged from the cold. It was beautiful and wild. It was easy to see why other people were drawn to settle here, and if I'd heard the slightest sigh of a suggestion that I might do the same, I'd have called a real estate agent.

But all was quiet. I wasn't home, and I wasn't wearing ruby slippers. We went to bed, and the next morning, following Tom's suggestion, we took a narrow dirt road heading northeast out of the valley. It wasn't on our map, and even Tom wasn't sure exactly where it led, but we could see it winding up into the mountains, and that was enough. "After all," Mark said, "We do have four-wheel drive."

We made slow progress through the stones and ruts that formed the road bed, and, as usual, I couldn't help fretting about whether we'd make it to civilization in one piece. Somehow, I was back on the cliff side, and I was still chafing against real-life adventure.

After an hour or so, we stopped in a wide spot to assess our progress. The valley lay behind and below us, serene and still. The air was cold, but the wind was no more than a breeze. A light winter sun hung above us, and the sky was pure cloud-less blue. We just stood there looking, and suddenly a big bird flew between us and the sun, so close we could feel the beat of his wings. "It's a hawk," said Mark.

The hawk was gone as swiftly as it appeared, and we stood standing, gazing out at the huge vacant sky. I expected my familiar yearning to surface again, my longing for home. Is this the place? Should I stop here? I waited for the questions to rise, but, was it the view, the hawk, my recent terror of hurtling off a cliff in the middle of nowhere? I don't know what happened, but somehow, up there in the Sangre de Cristos, that forbidding agglomeration of ancient stones, my questions blew away on a winter wind.

In their place was a simple answer. "You're home already," a quiet voice seemed to say. "You're where you're supposed to be, at this perfect juncture of time and space. That's what home is, sweetheart."

It really was as simple as that. I've been home ever since, no matter where my body is taking up space. The less stuff I own, and the less spread out it is, the bigger the area that feels like home. If that sounds like a paradox, well, I guess it is. But since that morning in the mountains above Angel Fire, I haven't once wondered where my home was hiding. Since that day, it's been always with me.

Always Home

Do you have any idea how simply splendid it is to be always home? It had taken me a year, but suddenly I could revel in the blissful simplicity of existing in just one spot. All at once I understood how Jesus could enjoy living with only one coat. He wasn't deprived. He had the luxury of needing no closet.

I had the luxury of needing no purse. Since purses are the security blankets of American women, this may seem more like punishment that privilege, but for me, it was a lovely freedom. For nearly three decades, I'd never been without my personal luggage, my portable repository for all the things I simply couldn't do without while I was away from home. Of course, this invariably meant I was packing a bunch of trash along with the useful items: old receipts, ticket stubs, worn-out pens, candy wrappers, loose change, odd keys, the detritus of everyday life.

And I could never stop worrying about losing the damn thing. It was like a body part that wasn't attached well enough, like a foot that you could leave in a bus if you weren't careful. And losing it was a dreaded thing, especially if you happened to be far away from home. Purse loss was a major topic of conversation when I was a college student on a semester abroad in Italy. The repartee was always the same.

"I lost my boat ticket in Athens."

"I can top that. I lost my passport in Naples."

"That's nothing. All my money and my train ticket back to London got stolen on the Paris Metro."

"No, wait. I lost my whole purse in Vienna."

"Oh my god."

For American women, and the fear starts young, losing a purse is far worse than losing a boyfriend, bone mass, or an ozone layer.

And now I'd lost mine permanently, and I was thrilled. I still don't own one, don't carry one, don't want one. It's my truest symbol of freedom. Maybe someday I won't even need pockets. It's something to strive for, but right now I still need a place for loose change.

But I'm hardly a Buddha. Enlightened souls don't tote toilets. That's reserved for people like Queen Elizabeth, who, I've been told, brings her own loo wherever she goes. It's not that she's hoity toity. It's just that she's not amused by the notion of seeing a toilet seat hanging on a wall some day, bearing the label, "Queen Elizabeth sat here."

It's comforting to know that I'm protected from similar embarrassment. I, too, carry a loo of my own. For people who don't know better, my lifestyle may not seem privileged, but consider this. In the last five years, I've warmed far fewer strange commodes than your typical suburban BMW owner. I ask you, who's more aristocratic, a woman with her own private water closet in tow, or a guy in an Armani suit who stops to pee at McDonald's?

And I'm not selfish about it. I share my facilities with those less fortunate. Come to think of it, my own toilet seat has been graced by derrieres glamorous enough to warrant my hanging it on a wall. But don't you worry, oh noted ones. You're lucky that I have better taste in home decor, and no wall space to spare anyway.

Lots of people who choose the mobile life tow cars behind their motorhomes, or pull trailers with pick-up trucks. They arrive at preselected destinations, set up housekeeping, and use the smaller vehicles as satellites. "Why don't you tow a car?" these well-wheeled ones often ask. "It's so handy for errands."

Errands. The word alone is enough to make me foreswear cars forever, just like purses. It reeks of endless aisles and dull routine. Errands wear ruts in your life, the same way commutes do. Errands and commutes mean going back as often as you go forward. They rack up miles, but at the end of a thousand, you still haven't gotten anywhere.

In our first four years, Mark, Marvin and I covered 115,000 miles. The odometers of most Los Angeles professionals would reflect the same number in the same amount of time. The difference is that the wheels of the commuter run over familiar tracks, back and forth, to and fro.

I know. For ten years, I was the quintessence of the Southern California job holder. I drove thirty miles each way to work, crawling in the same direction as thousands of other coffee-drinking minions each morning. Every evening I'd crawl back with the same horde, and on Saturdays we all went on the same errands, filling giant suburban parking lots with row after glistening row of our four-wheeled exoskeletons.

I never minded "to", but I got sick unto death of "fro." "Forth" would have been fine, but "back" became anathema. Life in the Phoenix was all to's and forth's. Our paths drew triangles and squares and circles on maps, but we never created the heavy over-and-over lines of our former lives. Why, when it had been so blissful to give it up, would I want to set up a place to which I had to wear a path? And why, in the name of all I held good, would I want to require myself to own a purse?

You need a purse only if you have a here and a there. I want only a here, with no such word as errand necessary. If, as the road unrolls beneath me, I need food or raiment, I know I'll find it along the way. There is no dearth of shops and grocers on the road to the horizon.

So no car follows the Phoenix as we ply the road. As Mark says, "With a car back there, we might as well not have four-wheel-drive. We'd have to leave it somewhere if we wanted to go off-road. And then we'd have to go back and get it."

Neither of us wanted back or there or then. We wanted forth and here and now. One truck was enough, and there are times when even it seems excessive. There are times I'd like to travel even lighter, with one coat, one pair of shoes. There are times when, having found the pleasure of owning no purse, I'd like to plumb the possibilities inherent in needing no closet.

But you know, I really have nothing against commutes and errands and daily routine. It's never the action that wears the rut in your soul. It's whether the action is getting you where you want to go. The deed is only dull when it isn't cutting its way to your heart's desire.

Our life had its full complement of routine. If you travel with a toilet, you can't ignore the inexorably expanding contents of your holding tank. If you want to make tracks, you can't ignore the inexorably shrinking contents of your gas tank. If your heart's desire is to send e-mail from the hinterlands, you try and try and try again.

I was, as ever, filing a story every week with the newspaper in California, and digital communion was still an elaborate ritual. If we were in the mountains, we'd drive from ridge to ridge, watching the cellular phone all the while. When the signal strength reached the minimum necessary for a successful connection, we'd screech to a halt. There was no such thing as logging on while rolling.

And success wasn't dictated merely by signal. Back in 1994, cellular telephone companies were still figuring out how to offer nationwide service, which, since it required cooperation among a score of local companies, took as much negotiation and diplomacy as it took to create Yugoslavia. Customers paid for the whole enterprise in the form of 'roam' charges. If you wanted the luxury of using a cellular telephone outside of your access provider's bailiwick, you had to pay through the nose. A human operator was often employed to make connections, and payment by credit card was required.

Making a single telephone call could take as much as twenty minutes of negotiation, which would have been inconvenience enough, but for our purposes, it spelled disaster. It had taken all my powers to pummel my software into working with the cellular phone under optimal conditions. I hadn't the faintest idea how to figure the interruption of a human voice into the equation, and, lest you think I'm above asking for help from superior beings, no computer whiz I could find knew what to do either.

All of this meant that in New Mexico, our cellular telephone was a useless hunk of black plastic. It wouldn't work at all, and no ancient magic could help. To file my story in the land of enchantment, I had to hire the services of an antediluvian fax machine. The deed accomplished, we went to Texas.

· 12 ·

Life Among the Peccaries

Arizona Detour

Y ou just never know what Americans will be thinking when you say "Texas" to them. Some think "big," and some think "bigoted." Some think "oil," and some think "cattle." Lots think "Dallas," the television show, and some think "Dallas," the city that killed Kennedy.

I used to think "forever" when I heard the word, because that's how long it seemed to take to drive across it. But that was before I learned that boredom doesn't grow in surroundings. It flourishes in the agar of your own soul. Which means I have to take you on a detour to Arizona before I return to Lone Star territory.

Before I set out on a never-ending journey that had no stated purpose, no itinerary, and no destination, touring the United States had always been a connect-the-dots operation. The dots were points of interest, and the lines connecting them were long, tedious are-we-there-yet highways with faceless, boring towns scattered along their edges. Since, with fore-knowledge derived from travel guides, the auto club and previous junkets, I already knew which places were interesting, what was the point in exploring the others unless I needed a drink, a burger, or a toilet?

One such place was Gila Bend, Arizona, a town I'd passed through many a time on many a dot-connecting journey. It's out in the desert somewhere between Phoenix and the California border, and it usually appears through your windshield when you're getting thirsty, hungry, or need to pee.

Since I had already relegated the place to my boring list, my heart fluttered not when Gila Bend rose on the sand in front of the Phoenix. We would have left it in the dust without another thought, but it was eight o'clock and about to get dark when we reached the town limits. "I guess we'll be spending the night in Dullsville," I said.

I pulled out the fat, dog-eared directory of campgrounds we kept handy for such exigencies, and one establishment was listed. "It doesn't sound lovely," I said, "But all we're going to do is sleep and leave, so who cares?"

The campground was wedged between an abandoned Mexican restaurant and a junkyard. A dusty trailer had a shingle nailed on the door that said "office." Inside, a woman with so many children she didn't know what to do assigned us a campsite. "Have fun!" she called as she rushed off in pursuit of a grubby two-year-old whose diaper had fallen off. "You betcha!" I did not call after her.

The sun had just set by the time we'd parked, and Mark took Marvin outside to survey the landscape and look for bushes. They were back in five minutes.

"There's a Christmas tree here," he said, "A tall one, covered with lights and ornaments." It was July, and the temperature was just drifting down from the three-digit range. A Christmas tree did seem a little out of place.

"I'm going to go take a closer look," said Mark. "Want to come?"

As a matter of fact, I did not want to come. I wanted to ignore the whole dingy place, Christmas trees, dirty babies and all. I wanted to go to sleep, wake up, and hit the road.

"Sure," I said anyway. "Let me put on my shoes."

The growing darkness improved our surroundings. Warm lights glowed from ramshackle trailers, and the Christmas tree actually looked quite lovely. It was a tall fir tree, and someone had persevered in attaching lights and ornaments all the way up to its topmost branches.

A leathery, bearded man clad in nothing but shorts was sitting in a folding chair between the tree and a silver bullet-shaped trailer. He was drinking beer out of a long-necked bottle, and he smiled as we approached. "Hey," he said amiably. "I'm Tim."

"I'm Mark," said Mark, "And this is Megan. We saw your tree when we arrived, and we came over to take a closer look."

"Hey, I've been working on this thing ever since I moved here four years ago. People give me stuff to hang on it." All kinds of stuff, I noted. In one glance I saw a naked Barbie doll, a teddy bear made out of old panty hose, a pair of peace symbol earrings, some sequined sunglasses and a paper airplane.

"Your first time in Gila Bend?" Tim asked. "I'm from Michigan, but I just can't leave a place where I can dress like this every day of the year. He stretched lazily and scratched his tanned belly. "It's paradise."

"And it has loads of history," Tim added suddenly. He jumped up and disappeared inside his trailer. In a few minutes, he returned carrying a yellowed newspaper.

"Look at this," he said, unfolding it. "Burt Reynolds committed a murder here." We peered down at the aging tabloid in front of us. Sure enough, Gila Bend had hit the big time when Burt stayed in one of the local motels while he was making a movie back in the seventies. In his spare time, the yellowed rag reported, he'd created a large ruckus with his co-star, a local motel owner, and a dead body.

Tim looked at our faces expectantly. "I can show you the motel if you like. I know the owner."

Noticing that we weren't responding with alacrity, he quickly changed tack. "John Wayne owned a ranch near here," he said.

"What about ostriches?" asked Mark, in an effort to shift the topic away from movie stars and corpses. "We were looking for an ostrich ranch in California, but we never found it. Are there any around here?"

A big grin spread over Tim's face. "Do we got ostriches," he said. "I have a friend who has a whole herd. Lemme call him up tomorrow and see when I can bring you over."

Tim sat down again. "Want a beer?" he said. "Or a toke?"

We thanked him anyway and said we'd drop by in the morning.

"Just before we blow this place," I whispered to Mark as we walked back to the Phoenix.

"Look at that," said Mark, ignoring me. He was pointing at a large vehicle that looked like a horse trailer. "But it has windows," said Mark. "I think it's a bunkhouse. Look at the other trucks parked near it. There's a story behind that setup, too."

Oh, god, I thought. Not another one. But Mark stayed with me. We ate some cold spaghetti and went to bed.

In the morning, which arrived with typical desert abruptness, we had just sat down to coffee, when there was a knock on the door. It was Tim, accompanied by a man in denim overalls.

"Hey, this is Ken," he said. "He's the ostrich farmer, and he says it's okay if we go out there later. I told him two o'clock, if that's okay with you."

"It's great," said Mark. "It's fabulous," I echoed. And they were gone.

"And now you have time to check out the rolling bunkhouse," I said.

"You read my mind," Mark replied. He was smiling, and I sighed.

"We might as well sign up for another night here," I said. "By the time we get through with the ostriches, we won't want to drive anywhere else." I was still nonplused at the thought of staying two nights in a five-minute burg. But I had to admit, Dullsville was growing more interesting by the minute, and the day was young.

You know the rest. Gila Bend just sat there, but I couldn't. I had to visit some ostriches, go for a ride in a combine as it cut wheat on a ranch once owned by John Wayne, and admire Tim's project, a pickup truck made entirely out of parts scavenged from junk heaps.

"My rule is that I can't pay for anything," he said as he ran his hand over the Ford fender and the Chevy hood. "My partners and I are willing to wait." His partners, Brooks and Beanie, were both well into their eighties.

Three days after we'd pulled into Gila Bend, we made preparations to depart. Tim came over to say good-bye.

"This is for you," he said, holding out a fat marijuana cigarette. "I made it this morning, and it's all bud. No stems. No seeds."

Thanks anyway," said Mark, "But . . ."

"Thank you, Tim," I said, interrupting. "It's incredibly nice of you. Are you sure you want to part with it?"

"I made it for you," he said simply.

I took the gift and thanked him again. We bade him farewell and said we'd stop by the next time we found ourselves in Gila Bend.

"He would have been crushed if we hadn't taken it," I said as I put the joint in an envelope. Mark pushed it to the back of the small safe in which we kept passports and money. We forgot about it until a border guard searched the Phoenix at the Canadian border half a year later.

He didn't find it, but as we stood there waiting, I knew Gila Bend was laughing. "Call me boring, will you?" she called, and I answered, "Never again."

The Queen of the Starlight Theater

And Texas isn't boring, either, especially along its endless border with Mexico. Border zones are fascinating once you look beyond fond cartographic truth. On a map, Mexico's orange, the U.S. is green, and a thin black line separates the two with knife-edge simplicity. On a map, no blurred edges are allowed.

Maps are "Leave It To Beaver" optimists, jolly pictures of a world unsullied by real people. They don't reflect the three-dimensional consequences of thin black lines. The penciled edges of man-made tectonic plates bump and chafe each other with tremors equal to any natural cataclysm. Even in their quieter moments, border zones are resting volcanoes. They bubble and boil with an energy irresistible to revolutionaries, iconoclasts, and people who don't like rules.

If Mexico's orange and the U.S. is green, then Big Bend should be the brown you'd get from blending the two. Mix a little gunpowder into the pigment, and you'd get even closer to the three-dimensional truth. Big Bend's a wild place, and black lines have yet to tame it.

It's a Janus-faced space with escape hatches in both directions and a strange calm in the middle where last names are optional and the only useful currency is cold, hard cash. Big Bend is the quintessence of interstitial frontier, right up there with the Conch Republic of Key West and the secret forests between Maine and New Brunswick. It's one of the delightful blurry places cartographers don't have symbols to represent, an unbridled place that laughs in the face of political boundaries.

Part of the reason Big Bend stays unfettered is that it's not on the way to anywhere else. Interstate 10 and the Rio Grande part company just east of El Paso, where the river takes a southerly route to the Gulf, and the highway makes a long straight beeline for San Antonio. To get back to the river on a paved surface, you have to choose one of the two-lane tentacles that run south from the Interstate. You have to keep driving for 150 miles. You'd have to be a persevering fool to get to Terlingua, Lajitas or Study Butte by accident.

Another factor that keeps this triangular appendix uniquely free from outside interference is that the entire place is unmitigated Chihuahuan desert, an arid expanse that sleeps during the day and buzzes with activity when the sun goes down.

The action starts at dusk, as we discovered the afternoon we arrived. We climbed a low ridge to watch the sun set over the Chisos Mountains, and as the evening darkened, we heard sounds in the underbrush. We waited, and soon a platoon of slick-bristled peccaries marched out of a tamarisk grove. They trampled and rooted and chewed their way across the hillside on their cloven, high-heeled hooves. Even cactus wasn't safe from their leathery snouts and tough little maws. Snuffling and grunting, they plundered a General Sherman swath through a dense stand of prickly pears and laid waste to a creosote grove.

Wild peccaries are no bigger than barnyard shoats, but what they lack in size, they make up for in smell. A musky stench rushes ahead of them to announce their advent, travels with the pack, and leaves more than a memory when they've passed. Humans, eyes watering, reel at the pungency, but for dogs, it's a siren call. Marvin threw himself against his collar, strangling and whining with the desperate infatuation I'd heretofore seen him display only in the presence of anchovy pizza. The peccaries, like prom queens walking past a Cub Scout, ignored him.

I was enchanted but not surprised at the alarm clock effect that sundown had on the Rio Grande. Desert fauna is nocturnal by nature, as anyone who's ever spent time in arid climes is well aware. It was the desert humanity that surprised me.

Terlingua was a ghost town by day, a deserted settlement built in the late 1800s to support a quicksilver mining operation. A quiet gift store and a booking office for river guides were the only signs of life at high noon.

At night, all that changed. The Starlight Theater opened its doors, and the gravelly hillside filled with trucks and Jeeps. The bar inside was jammed with tanned men in cowboy boots, river guides in canvas shorts, and an entourage I guessed were tourists who'd spent the day in the Mexican border town of Ojinaga. They were wearing bright new serapes and stiff unweathered leather hats. Dinner was being served by candlelight on wooden tables at one end of the room, and at the other, musicians were setting up equipment on a stage. Mark and I elbowed our way up to the bar, where we were flanked by a bronzed Adonis in a nylon mesh shirt and one of the serape-clad tourists.

The god next to Mark had just returned from a kayak run, and my neighbor hailed from Los Angeles. The serape-clad retinue of which he was a member had just finished shooting a movie called "Streets of Laredo," and tomorrow, they'd be heading home.

In the meantime, they were in a mood to cause a tequila drought in Big Bend. Several were swigging straight from bottles, and Vince, the one I was standing next to, had already drunk himself into a state of blubbery pathos.

As I stood there listening to Vince's woes, tales of death by white water filtered in from the other side. Three Mexican caballeros were joking boisterously in Spanish nearby, and a city slicker in dude ranch duds kept nudging his way up to the bar for shots of peppermint schnapps. It was noisy and smoky and packed, and I half expected Matt Dillon to sidle up beside me.

Forgive me, but I did. I found myself on a fringe where fiction and reality had moved in together, a remnant of a wild west so thoroughly represented in letters and film that it was impossible to tell where romantic invention gave way to actuality.

The action filmed by the Hollywood movie makers might be staged fantasy, but the fight Vince was ripening for was all too real. The denizens of the Starlight Theater weren't actors, at least not now that the movie was in the can.

Vince's whiny tears had turned to drunken belligerence, and the cowboy next to him was not amused. I was beginning to think it might be time to retire to the Phoenix when a woman appeared at Vince's side. She was graceful and tall and wearing a low-cut knit top that advertised her breasts with understated flamboyance. She had steel gray curls and a proprietary air. My god, I thought. Maybe there's no Marshall Dillon in these parts, but if that's not Miss Kitty, I'm a wild peccary.

Miss Kitty, whose name we found out later was Angie Dean, was indeed the owner of the Starlight Theater. As we discovered in subsequent visits to her establishment, she presided at the far side of the bar, keeping one eye on the till and the other on time bombs like Vince. The instant he moved from lugubrious to bellicose, she was at his side.

She took the drink from his hand and whispered something in his ear. Immediately, his truculence dissolved into tears. "Come on, let's dance," said Angie, taking his hand. Vince followed obediently, his stiff serape encasing him with all the grace of a cardboard box.

I watched them dance, Aphrodite and baby Eros. She was mother and madam, and her attentions meant that Vince's nose, Angie's bottles, and our evening remained unbroken by violence. I watched her resume her throne on the far side of the bar after depositing a semi-conscious Vince on a bench by the door. She reined all evening with steely elegance, and it was easy to tell which patrons were regulars. Not a one ordered a drink without first paying homage to the queen of the Starlight Theater.

Mañanaland

We spent the next few days exploring the wild expanses and canyons of Big Bend. At night we mingled with the human wildlife, discovering such hideaways as the Kiva, an underground lair whose patrons seemed to have no names, need no passports, pay no taxes, and take no prisoners.

One night we stopped at a well-lit house with a sign out front that said "Desert Opry." Inside, we found an art gallery, a restaurant, and a family: Alice, Jack and Alice's son Arjuna. Alice was a songwriter and painter. Jack, who cooked us dinner, was a guitarist, and Arjuna spent most of his time going to and from high school in Alpine. "It's a hundred miles each way," he said. "The longest school bus run in America. We get on the bus at five a.m., and they won't let us bring blankets. They're afraid something between the boys and girls might go on under them. But anyway, I'm going to finish high school by correspondence. I've only got one more year."

Alice told us how Big Bend's population was largely regulated by water and who owned the rights. Land was plentiful, but a good well was hard to find. "That's what the locals spend most of their time arguing about," she said. "We're pretty much self-governed. You don't see a state trooper down this way more often than once a week, sometimes less."

"They don't really think of this as Texas," added Jack. "It's not Mexico, though. Mexico's definitely over there." He gestured in a southerly direction. "This right here, well, we call it Mañanaland. We even wrote a song about it. Are you ready to hear it?"

We'd finished eating, and it was time for the live music to begin. It didn't matter that we were the only customers that evening, because Alice, Jack and Arjuna sang to us as though we were a full house. Suddenly I understood what had been behind crazy King Ludwig's self-indulgence when he built his private theater at Linderhof in Bavaria. It's an ersatz cave, complete with a huge lake and a stage grand enough for no-holds-barred Wagner. "And bitte look at zis," the guide says. "Ze viewing balcony has chairs only for six." Insane he may have been, but Ludwig wasn't crazy in thinking that private concerts are wonderful things. Alice sang songs she'd written, and Jack and Arjuna played guitar and drums.

As always, we were running out of money, and we'd even debated about eating in a restaurant when we had a perfectly good can of chili sitting in our cupboard. "I think we've got enough cash," Mark had said, "If we have only one thing to drink."

We did have enough to cover the numbers on the check that Jack brought us before we left, but it wasn't enough to pay for a priceless evening. It certainly wasn't enough to nudge Alice's Nashville hopes toward reality or relieve Arjuna of his 200-mile commute. We weren't the only ones with dreams to fund.

"Will you take a check?" Mark asked. "We're running low on cash, and you don't seem to have any banks in these parts. Nobody seems to like credit cards around here, either."

"A check'll be fine," said Jack. "But you're right. Big Bend operates on a cash basis. All cash, no questions asked. That's how it is in Mañanaland."

Mark pulled out a check, and I watched him fill in an amount that left enough in our account to buy one tank of gas. It was a heck of a tip.

"The best things in life are free," he said as we drove away, "Except for the ones that cost everything you've got."

"Dreams are cheap," I replied. "It's making them come true that eats up the bucks. And it's a good thing we have that can of chili in the cupboard."

And so we found ourselves once again down to our penultimate nickel, our terminal dime. The next morning we searched our pockets for forgotten change. I found a twenty-dollar bill in my winter jacket, and we were flush again. We could spend our last evening in Mañanaland at the Starlight Theater.

But Big Bend wouldn't let us off the hook quite so easily. For starters, D-day arrived, and the D stood for deadline. I had a story to file, and cellular signals were rarer than high schools in Mañanaland. This was before Website mania had swept the land, and the natives were as suspicious of electronic gadgets as they were of credit cards and people who used them. Even pay phones were scarce, but there was one at the ranger station in the national park. I decided that the situation called for intervention by Iguana.

"Fat chance it'll work," I said to Mark as we stood in front of the telephone. "Big Bend Telephone Company" read the placard affixed to the front. It was a model so basic, I half expected an operator to greet me when I picked up the receiver.

"Well, there's a dial tone," I said. "It's a weird one, but I'm willing to give it a try."

It was broad daylight, which meant Mark had to hold an umbrella over my head as I balanced the notebook computer on my knees and squinted at the screen. With the Iguana lashed onto the receiver with its Velcro straps, I began the elaborate ritual of dialing the access number and entering my credit card account numbers with timing I hoped would appease the modem gods.

Danged if it didn't work the first time. My computer listened politely to the static issuing from the telephone and responded by transferring the file I had asked it to send. It even collected my new e-mail and logged off without expletive or violence on my part. I smiled at Mark around the umbrella. "This may be Mañanaland, but I met my deadline with hours to spare." One more time, the electronic express had gotten the mail through. Even among the peccaries, I hadn't had to resort to a fax machine.

The day was young, and my success with the Iguana made me want to seize it with alacrity. When we came to a crossroads and saw one sign that said "Hot Springs," and another that said "Unsafe for Large Vehicles," I was the one who said, "Oh, that's just to warn wimps in Winnebagos. With four-wheel drive we'll make it, no problem." Mark, in a switch of roles, had initially balked but said at last, "Well, okay, what the heck?"

By the time we sat down at the Starlight bar, we considered ourselves fortunate to be there. The road I'd been so cockily sure would accommodate our behemoth was no more than a rocky ledge along a deep ravine. Not only was it too narrow and unstable for large vehicles, it was no picnic for Jeeps. A rock wall bulged alarmingly on one side, and the crevasse yawned on the other. I had an unbroken view out the cliff side window as eight tons of Phoenix leaned ominously over the edge.

"But hey, we didn't fall," said Mark. "Let's drink to the wonderfulness of 'not quite.'" "You mean like running out of money?" I asked, clanking my margarita against his. "We haven't yet. Not quite."

Not quite. Can you fathom the unbelievable power of those words? I've lived on them ever since, because after a week in Big Bend, I began to notice that the walls I'd been the most afraid of hitting weren't the rocky ones on the edges of wild ravines. The ones I'd spent my life fearing were nothing more than a mime's creation, an invisible surface traced out by convincing hands for a willing audience. When I stretched my own hands forth to feel the stones and know the limits of my universe, blow me down if I didn't keep right on moving. Either the stones were made of smoke, or they weren't there at all.

And so we bade farewell to Big Bend, that place of wonder that is not quite Mexico, not quite Texas, not quite civilized, not quite safe. We hadn't quite run out of money, gas, food, or even rocky ledge. Even the Iguana had cooperated, and I hadn't quite missed a deadline. Not quite, and life was good.

· 13 ·

Location, Location, and Gnats

Miraculous Cure By Optical Illusion

After we bade farewell to the peccaries, the Rio Grande and the Starlight Theater, we headed north. We turned east at a place appropriately called Junction and set our sights on Dixieland. As a tiny child, I'd lived briefly in Virginia, but as an adult, my real-life exposure to the American South was limited to a week in the Smoky Mountains.

It had been a perfect destination. I had just concluded my own civil war, and, divorce final, I wanted the taste of new surroundings. I flew to Atlanta and emerged from the airport in the only vehicle the rental agency had available. A suitable witness to my midlife Appomattox, it was a red sports car. Foot to the floor and radio blasting, I drove north into Tennessee, into a universe of tourist traps and dulcimer music and mountains covered with rhododendrons.

I did it all. I filled my carpet bags at Pigeon Forge factory stores and drank Jack Daniel's in Gatlinburg night clubs. I hiked through the clouds to the top of Mount LeConte, and I rode a raft down Nantahala rapids. It was a week of glorious reconstruction.

Otherwise, my acquaintance with the south was drawn from *Gone With the Wind* and the nightly news. If Georgia was ever on my mind at all, she was antebellum splendor, and Mississippi was a scratchy newsreel of civil rights marches. Louisiana was nothing but Mardi Gras, and Florida was where the boys were. Alabama? Arkansas? Red mud and overalls. I'd traveled the world, but I was an ignorant Yank when it came to Dixie.

We came to a halt in Birmingham. The Phoenix One's brakes had failed, and we spent three days in a Ford truck garage, reading old magazines and talking to Jewel, the bookkeeper, and Mark, a truck salesman. Jewel loaned us her car so we could have lunch at a nearby mall, and Mark told us how Alabama wasn't as boring as the surface suggested.

"We don't have much in the way of mountains," he said, "But we've got caves to make up for it." When he ran out of spelunking tales, he regaled us with stories about people who'd been miraculously healed by looking at optical illusions. Even so, the hours crawled.

"Your mechanic is good, but he's slow," said Mark, summing everything up on the third day. "I sure hope you didn't need to be somewhere."

"In fact, we don't need to be anywhere," I said, but I realized I'd been acting like it, making it clear that anywhere but where I was would be an improvement, and that three days in a Birmingham truck garage was nigh on close to hell. Our hosts had been apologetic, but I was the one who should have been saying I was sorry. Where did I need to be, after all? Nowhere but where I was. Jewel had cleared a table for me in the office lobby. I had my computer, unlimited quantities of coffee, a comfortable chair, and even a good story teller to keep me company.

Suddenly I saw things differently. One minute my surroundings were oil-encrusted purgatory, but when I looked again, danged if it wasn't the nicest sort of spot. It was nothing less than a miraculous cure by optical illusion, and, almost as soon as it occurred, the Phoenix was ready to roll. Bidding farewell to Jewel and Mark, we drove north on Interstate 65, and turned east at Decatur. We were headed to Huntsville.

A Little Graveyard On The Moon

Huntsville, which before 1940 was merely the "Watercress Capital of the World," burgeoned in the post-war years to become the home of NASA's Marshall Space Flight Center, the U.S. Space and Rocket Center, and U.S. Space Camp. Redstone Arsenal, the army installation which had built missiles for the war effort, provided the land. No longer a little green hamlet dozing in the hills, Huntsville is Rocket City, and the first thing we saw when we drove in from the west was a life-size mockup of the space shuttle.

The first famous foreigner to be connected with Huntsville was the English poet Alexander Pope, and the town even enjoyed a brief spell under the name of Twickenham, Pope's English home. Nowadays, Huntsville might well be renamed to honor another European, Wernher Von Braun. Germany's premier rocket scientist came to Alabama in 1950 and never looked back. Thanks largely to him, Sputnik, and the launching of the space race, Huntsville never looked back either. You can find the remnants of antebellum splendor if you look, but postwar space mania holds the day.

After we parked in the small campground located in a grove of trees next to the Space & Rocket Center, we hooked Marvin to his leash and set out to explore. The Center was already closed for the day, but it was easy to see the larger artifacts of Rocket Park through the chain link fence. An impressive stand of missiles rose like a stately grove of limbless trees.

We skirted the perimeter, and our attention was quickly drawn away from the carefully preserved specimens inside the fence. All around us were shards and fragments of nose cones and fuselages, propellers and fins, a thousand decaying remnants of the space race, half-hidden in the grass. Some were covered with kudzu vines, soon to be lost under a veil of green. The chariots of the space pioneers rested in this silent cemetery, and we picked our way through their rusting remains as darkness closed in around us.

A full moon rose as we walked back to the Phoenix. "There's a graveyard up there, too," I said pointing. "A little pile of human debris that proves to alien archaeologists that the moon once hosted visitors from another world."

"It seems so long ago," said Mark, "So long that the machines that made it happen look like the ancient relics of a dead civilization. I wonder what happened. Why hasn't anyone returned?"

It was a good question. Didn't we all assume back in 1969 that within a few years humans would be making regular voyages to the moon or even living there? Now that the barrier had been broken, what was stopping us? Soon there would be commercial flights and domed colonies and business ventures and even holiday space cruises. Humans had gone the distance and made it back alive. Anything was possible. Certainly no one dreamed that we'd greet the new millennium with no more than the same little pile of litter on our very own satellite.

But what did we know? Technology doesn't always grow in a straight line, as I was reminded every time I prayed to the modem gods and thanked the black box for its efforts at cellular data transfer. It's trimmed and shaped by politics and circumstance, espaliered by fad and necessity. Maybe the conquest of the moon was an ego trip, inspired by nothing more than a rabid desire to be the first to plant a flag on extraterrestrial soil. Maybe it was nothing more than a Cold War campaign, designed to intimidate our enemies and rally support on the home front. Maybe the moon was as frivolous a goal as our desire for true mobile communication. Once achieved, maybe it had been tarred with the lethal brush of "No Viable Commercial Application."

"Maybe we'll find out more tomorrow," I said. "This is the place if anywhere is."

Give Me Screaming Frogs

The next morning, we arrived at the main entrance of the Space & Rocket Center just as the guard was opening the doors. "You were wise to come early," he said as he waved us inside. "You'll have it to yourselves until the school buses start to arrive."

We worked our way through the exhibits inside, and then headed out to Rocket Park, the outdoor museum we'd seen through the fence the evening before. By the end of the day, we'd toured Redstone Arsenal and visited Space Camp. We'd walked through the history of American space travel and admired the latest project at Marshall Space Flight Center, the International Space Station. We'd gazed up at triumphs like the Saturn V that blasted astronauts to the moon, and we'd stared at relics from Apollo 13, the ill-fated mission that nearly ended in disaster.

We'd watched children bounce in seats designed to show them the effects of lunar gravity, and observed others wearing lab coats as they experimented in a "clean room." We'd peered into the large water tank that provides astronauts a simulated weightless environment, and we'd walked through the forest of missiles, rockets, and supersonic planes.

We expected all that, of course, but we weren't expecting another curious thing. Behind everything we saw there seemed to lurk the presence of Wernher von Braun, the man who built the rockets that bombed London, the man most responsible for the footprints on the moon. Surrounded by stunning technological achievement, I was struck with the astonishing accomplishments of the man with the camera-ready smile.

"He reminds me of Walt Disney," I said to Mark as we looked at the shrine to his memory in the museum. "He had bigger dreams than most mortals and the right combination of brains and charisma to pull them off."

In fact, Wernher von Braun knew Walt Disney, and he even served as a technical adviser for Disneyland's Tomorrowland and several Disney television productions. Wernher von Braun liked anyone who helped him promote his own penchant for shooting rockets into space, and he liked anyone who would promote space travel among the masses. His was an expensive vocation, and he needed the coffers of a super power and the blessings of its taxpayers to fund it.

That's why, in 1945, when it became clear that the status quo was no longer an option, Wernher and a hundred or so of his colleagues decided to surrender to the United States. Even though the Americans were happy to find this enormous mass of brain power falling into their laps, things weren't smooth sailing for the German missile geniuses. Detained for months after they arrived on American soil, they referred to themselves as POP's, or "Prisoners of Peace."

By 1950, Wernher von Braun had emerged in Huntsville and launched his illustrious career as an American hero. He had his share of detractors, of course, those who considered him little more than a long-distance war criminal and the worst kind of hypocrite.

But here's what I think. I think he wanted to shoot rockets into space, and he wanted that more than he wanted anything else, including kind thoughts and flattering epithets. He had not only the skill to design missiles, but the ability to find sponsors with the deepest pockets in the world. Once he'd sold them on his dreams, he knew how to keep them wanting more. Sputnik and the Cold War helped, but I have the sneaking feeling that Wernher von Braun made use of whatever events came his way. His trajectory was truer than a rocket, his destination as clear as the brightest moon. He had a burning desire.

I have no idea whether I would have liked the man, but I do have a weakness for someone who sees his path and follows it, whose laser-straight determination won't let him be sidetracked by mundane distractions, even big ones like World War II. The obstacles he conquered were enormous, and the money he need-ed to follow his dream was beyond imagination. He did it any-way, and from his example I drew a second wind.

My ambitions seemed so tiny next to his, my budget so small. I didn't need to travel to another world. All I wanted was access to this one. All I asked of communications technology was the very thing it promised, a life free of identity with a physical location, an address in the ether. I wanted to roam like Odysseus without being lost, travel without vanishing, sally forth without forsaking community.

It was the first time in the history of the planet that such a life could be contemplated. Before the birth of electronic mail and the rise of the Internet, a truly mobile life required the sac-rifice of connection. Living without an address was living on a fringe. It meant dropping out, escaping from the status quo, reneging on the picket-fence security deal Americans have with society. It connoted tax evasion, law breaking and anarchy. Such an existence carried Easy Rider appeal, but those who chose it for more than a summer or two got failing marks in citizenship.

A life of travel was a boy's life, too. Men were the rovers, the gadabout warriors who only wanted home when the going got tough, when they needed a back rub or a bandage. Girls were the hearth-tending Penelopes who kept the home fires burning, made calico quilts, baked peanut butter cookies. Until my adventuring spirit was released by fire, I'd led a corseted existence, a life of tight stays and shallow breathing. I bought curtains and made chicken soup. I wore panty hose and carried a purse. I hadn't hated it, but when it was gone, I knew I could never stuff myself back inside the girdle of my former life.

I'd burst forth, but whose path could I follow? Who had gone before me to show me the way? I was no hobo soldier. I couldn't trade nylons for camouflage fatigues, dishes for mess kits. I liked flowers and comforters and clean hair. I liked books and computers and cosy nights. I was no bungie jumper, mountain climber, jungle tamer. I had a hard enough time loving the cliff side.

But I did have a mission, and as I stood looking at the man who bridged the lunar gap, I saw clearly that I had no one to follow except others who had walked right off the map. It wasn't trappings that made the mission. It was the path, a path that wasn't there until the trailblazer defined it.

I wanted to be as close as next door and a thousand miles distant. I wanted the simplicity of life with no purse and the complexities of technology to make it possible. I wanted an all-American life packed up to go. I wanted an office on Flathead Lake, and a bedroom with a view of redwoods. I wanted to dine in the Blue Ridge Mountains and fall asleep to crashing Acadian surf. I wanted packs of wild peccaries and kudzu-covered nose cones. I wanted a back yard with oceans for fences and a family that circled the globe.

I wanted my life's journey to unroll in space as well as time, and my grail was the technology that would connect all the dots in the world with me, even when I was a moving target. If I could do it, I knew I wouldn't be the only one to relish the benefits. I couldn't be the only one whose heart beat faster at the thought of being at work, at home and on the road, all at the same grand moment.

I looked again at the man whom even a world war couldn't deter. He had known that his task went far beyond mere technological know-how. He'd been the salesman for the Apollo program, the cheerleader of the space race. It wasn't enough to design machines to do a job. Part of the innovator's task is to create the market, to ignite enthusiasm, to fan desire.

Why are there no new footprints on the moon? "Too expensive" is one answer we heard that day. "No need" is another. They were the same reasons Mark and I might logically have chosen to sell the Phoenix and rejoin the ranks of commuting suburbanites from which we'd sprung. What was the point of pursuing a truly mobile existence? Why try to fashion a complete life on the road? It's too expensive. There's no need. The ends of rainbows are for songs and simpletons.

If the pursuit of dreams is folly, then I was a first class fool. I'd spent a year learning how to survive on a roll, and, having achieved an acceptable level of competence in that arena, I'd progressed into genuine living. My former life had been centrifuged into compartments, each with a timeline, a wardrobe, a separate address. How could I return to that life of pigeonholes and labels when I had only begun to plumb the possibilities of an unsliced life? I liked having my whole life with me wherever I went. I'd learned the power of here and now. I'd caught a glimpse of the possibilities the virtual universe held for wanderers and dreamers and a woman without a purse. Expense and practicality be damned. I wanted a black box that really worked.

Mark jolted me out of my reverie. "I almost forgot to tell you," he said. "You know that little pond we discovered out where the space hardware is scattered in the grass? I took Marvin there for a walk this morning, and we discovered something amazing."

"What?" I asked, thinking immediately of lunar landers and rocket fins.

"The frogs who live there scream," said Mark. "They hear you coming, and they shriek. Then they jump in the water and hide."

Did I mention that I also want screaming frogs? I do. I want it all.

Splendor In The Swamp Grass

The screaming frogs of Huntsville were my first taste of the biotic ebullience of the American south. The mosquitoes in Arkansas were so big the natives celebrated them with an annual festival. I would have celebrated the fireflies, myself. They put on a nightly light show that beat any Sugar Plum fairy I ever saw. Woodchucks sat with twitching whiskers by the sides of roads, and squirrels the size of badgers darted in the pines.

At the other end of the spectrum were chiggers and tiny flying insects known as no-see-ums. The former lurked in shrubbery until a warm body passed nearby. Then they'd jump aboard, burrow under epidermal layers, and continue a life cycle that could be interrupted only by a thick application of nail polish to the affected areas.

"Ya gotta suffocate 'em," an Arkansan told us with the grim authority of experience. "Otherwise they keep secreting acid to dissolve your flesh, which they then slurp up. That's what itches." The nail polish remedy worked, although I'm happy to say I know this second hand. Mark had colonies in seven places after he climbed on the roof of the Phoenix while it was parked under a low hanging tree.

Chiggers were available any time, and mosquitoes emerged at dusk. No-see-ums and spiders attacked under cover of darkness, all of which meant there wasn't a moment in the summertime South when we stopped swatting or slapping or scratching.

But we didn't stop watching, either, and the fauna grew ever denser the farther we got down the long thumb of the Floridian peninsula. By the time we got to the Everglades, the water boiled, the land crawled, and the sky was dappled with birds.

One day, at that crepuscular hour that beasts love best, Mark, Marvin and I took a walk near Cypress Lake, not far from Orlando. In the gathering darkness, we caught sight of an armadillo in the grass. He was trundling along in his little suit of armor, oblivious to everything but the ground in front of his little pointed snout. Two humans and a dog were less than fifteen feet away, but the armadillo noticed not.

Marvin strained and struggled against his collar, eager to make the acquaintance of this plated oddity. The armadillo kept ambling along. He had the air of a carefree whistler, a creature on a safe, familiar path. He snuffled right up to our toes.

As he sniffed our toes, he drew back with the slightest of double takes. "Hmm," he seemed to comment to himself, "I do believe that's an unusual smell." Slowly, slowly, he turned his pointed face upward. At last he made eye contact, and for a split second, man, woman, dog and armadillo communed. Then a look of consummate terror exploded over his face. He turned, nearly rolled over in his fright, and fled.

We continued our walk and soon arrived at the edge of the lake. The surface was gray and opaque in the gathering dusk, rippling around the air boats and dinghies tied to the dock. We walked the length of the wooden structure and stood at the end. The air was still and humid.

"But the water keeps moving," said Mark. "I thought it was a breeze at first, but there isn't the slightest breath of one."

The water boiled and rippled with a life of its own, a secret submarine ecogalaxy that broke the surface every minute or two with the flick of a tail or the flash of a fin. Once, with sinister silence, the two saurian eyes of an alligator rose in front of us and just as quietly slipped back under the oily surface.

Near the bait shop was a pay phone lit by a single bulb. The light had attracted a fuzzy cloud of gnats so large and dense it rendered the telephone all but useless. "Unless you want a mouthful of insects every time you say something," I commented as we walked past.

And then I noticed the other tiny pilgrim at the telephone Mecca. It was a small frog, dazzling in its green iridescence. It was sitting on top of the telephone, and sure enough, every time it flicked out its tongue, it reeled it back in studded with a satisfying load of gnats.

"He doesn't even have to aim," I said. "He doesn't even have to try."

"He's got real estate with the three most important qualities, all right," said Mark. "Location, location, and gnats."

"I'm very grateful I don't have to use that telephone with my computer," I'd said. " I'd be debugging it for the rest of my life."

In the morning, the frog was gone, and a pile of dead gnats lay in a soft drift under the telephone. That night, the frog was back, amid an even bigger cloud of gnats. I like to think that shiny frog is still there every evening, huge now, a giant jewel of a toad, bloated on a lifetime of easy feasting.

We'd just come from Disney World, where gnats are anathema, and the alligators are made of plaster and fiberglass. When

Walt and his cronies came to Florida to carve out a fairy land in the jungle, their goal was to beat back the fauna as thoroughly as an asteroid wiped out the dinosaurs.

We spent a whole day in Epcot Center, and never once did I see so much as a fly. In the evening, back at a campground just outside the Disney ring of fire, we were blanketed with mosquitoes, and a pygmy rattlesnake struck at Mark and Marvin when they went for a walk off the pavement.

The plants are different inside the enchanted zone, too. In real Florida, there are strangler figs and tropical vines and grasses that cut through skin. In the Disney universe, everything is Cotswold borders and marigolds, velvet lawns and pink carnations. The imports love the sun, and all their enemies are kept at bay by battalions of uniformed gardeners and sophisticated insecticide delivery systems.

Disney keeps expanding the borders of its better-than-real-life enclave. We went back in 1997, and a town called Celebration had just opened. It's a manufactured city built on land reclaimed from swamp and marsh, just like the rest of the Disney empire. Its perfectly proportioned streets were lined with American dreams, storybook houses where Beaver and Donna Reed might spend happy days with a father who knows best. It had a darling main street, too, and a post office right out of Mayberry.

And no bugs. Not a one. No creepy vines, no snakes, and every hint that alligators once ruled had been erased and replaced with apple pie atmosphere imported from Kansas. I can't say it wasn't lovely. The houses and shops were so Johnny-comes-marching-home perfect I wanted to come back for Christmas and the Fourth of July. Celebration is a Norman Rockwell painting in three dimensions, and if you never stepped outside its boundaries, you could easily forget that it was built in a swamp.

And the swamp hasn't been beaten. It lurks around the edges of the Disney realm like an ever-wakeful Argus, waiting for its chance to send in a snake or dispatch an alligator. Celebration, like all the other Disney colonies in Orlando, is an alien fortress built on hostile ground. My eyes took pleasure in the happy verandas and jolly lawns, but they also saw the tropical wilderness lurking at the perimeter. Appearances to the contrary, the swamp things have made only a superficial retreat.

It was that tropical wilderness I found fascinating, not its momentary conquerors. The Disney dynasty is a temporary artifice, and it's not difficult to imagine the day when its ersatz mountains and plastic pirates will lie ruined in the swamps and marshes from which they rose, a fascinating conundrum for the archaeologists of the future.

Mai Tais With The Snowbirds

A day at Epcot Center and two nights at a campground ruled by a monolithic statue of Yogi Bear were enough to sate my appetite for cartoon-inspired environments. I was ready for a taste of what lay beyond the plaster and pavement. I was ready for alligators and anhingas and mangroves and manatees, for all the denizens of that intermediate zone that isn't really land and isn't really sea. We headed for the Everglades, even though it was the time of year when most people head north.

We skirted Lake Okeechobee, a giant circular depression with a perimeter defined by an endless border of trailers and motorhomes. There were gaps now and then created by the summer exodus, but a thick phalanx of breadbox dwellings remained, their wheels having long since rolled to a permanent halt. It was hot and quiet and moist, and we stopped overnight at the edge of Loxahatchee National Wildlife Reserve.

Actually, we stayed at Lion Country Safari, because theme parks have well-appointed campgrounds, and after a steamy day, I was ready for the cool, mosquito-free cocoon that 30 amp power could provide. Resort campgrounds usually offer cable television hookups, too, and industrial strength ice machines. Some have whirlpools and billiard tables in air-conditioned club-houses.

It's not surprising. They're built for retirees and vacationers, people who've earned the right to loll and bask and listen to Neil Diamond tapes in Polynesian bars. What right had I to take advantage of such amenities? At best I was a working stiff, and to many eyes, I looked like an undeserving dropout who hadn't bought enough nylons to merit a place in the sun.

But you know what? As much as I enjoyed my air conditioning that night, as much I liked lapsing into television-induced catatonia with an icy drink at my elbow, it wasn't enough. It was refreshing after a steamy day on the edge of the Everglades, but it was no rainbow's end. It held no motivational power over me. It didn't make me want to go to New York and get a fifty-year job with retirement benefits. My life just wasn't for sale on the usual terms any more. The big payoffs, house, car and golf course retirement now seemed less appealing than purse and panty hose.

Which isn't to say I didn't want to work. I just didn't seem to have the heart to labor for lucre and luxuries alone. I couldn't seem to get out of neutral for anything less than the real thing, work that made my heart sing. If I'd been a donkey, my master would have scratched his head. "That carrot on a string trick always worked with her," he'd say, "but it just doesn't get her going any more. Don't know what's come over her."

The next morning, we rolled on down Interstate 95, which follows the coast through places with names made famous by the movies: Palm Beach, Boca Raton, Fort Lauderdale. We sailed right by Miami and on down to Homestead, the last big town before land gives way to 'glade.

We had entered the zone where time isn't measured in years and decades, but rather in intervals between havoc-wreaking winds. Hurricane Andrew had ripped through Homestead in 1992, and residents had erected signs to mark spots where he displayed unusually vehement shows of force. If they aren't there today, it's because another child of Aeolus has blown them away and created new landmarks.

Trailer resorts abounded, and we parked in a spot recently vacated by a northbound snowbird. The park catered to tanned retirees wearing Hawaiian print shirts and rubber flip-flops. We looked pasty in comparison, and the Phoenix stood out like a crown roast at a vegetarian buffet.

It didn't stop us from joining the throng at the establishment's bar that night. Its Polynesian decor set a high standard. The roof was thatched with palm fans and inside the walls were festooned with weathered nets, cork floats, plastic leis and desiccated marine life. Carved coconuts and rustic totems filled every available surface, and the drinks all came with little paper parasols, even the beers.

The bartender was a friendly blonde woman who rang a

ship's bell every time someone gave her a tip. The bronzed sixty-ish couple next to us were wearing Hawaiian shirts and rubber flip-flops. Their smiles revealed that they were friendly, too.

"Where y'all from?" the man asked, a question I can't answer smoothly to this day. It's easiest to say, "Los Angeles," and let the conversation progress to drive-by shootings, smog and O.J. Simpson. It's simplest, but it makes me feel like a liar. I'm not from L.A. any more than I'm from Illinois, where my mother happened to be when I was born.

Mark filled the vacuum left by my pause. "We're always on the road," he said.

"Oh, full-timers," said the man, happy to find a pigeonhole that fit. "We are, too. We spend the winter down here, and then we pull our trailer up to Maine for the summer. We have a spot in a park near Freeport."

So Mark's answer is no better than mine, and maybe it's worse. Nothing is quite so irritating to him as to be labeled a "full-timer."

"I hate the term," he says. "If you live in a house, you're a person, but if you live in a motorhome, you're a "full-timer." I can't stand being defined by my domicile."

But the conversation in the Tiki bar had already wended its way down a familiar path, and the tanned couple was eager to chat. They loved August in Acadia, and Christmas among the palm trees.

"I pinch myself sometimes," said the woman. "I love my life so much I get to thinking I must be dreaming."

"I like Florida better than Maine," said the man. "For me, this is heaven, including this bar. And the music hasn't even started yet."

Here I was thinking that paper parasols and freeze-dried fish were treat enough, and there was more. I hardly had time to wonder whether we were in for a Don Ho look-alike or a Blue Hawaii Elvis when a short, fat man in black shorts and red suspenders appeared at the end of the bar.

"That's Ronnie," said our neighbor. "He's fantastic."

Ronnie was wearing a set of headphones with an attachment that positioned both a microphone and a harmonica in front of his mouth. A keyboard stuck out at a right angle from his waist, attached to his shoulders with a sturdy nylon harness. He was perspiring heavily, and his mass of black hair clung to his flushed forehead in damp tendrils.

Ronnie spoke, and no one within a forty-foot radius could do anything but shut up and listen. He was — how do the sound guys put it? — amped to the max.

"HELLO," he bellowed. "AND HOW ARE WE ALL TONIGHT?"

He repeated his question until we all shouted "FINE" loud enough to suit him. Ronnie was slowly making his way down the bar, and I knew where he was headed. He was obviously an audience participation kind of entertainer, and we were the new kids on the block.

"WHERE Y'ALL FROM?" he blasted when he slowed to a halt in front of us. This time I didn't pause. Bar singers with headphones don't want Zen answers. They want place names, pure and simple.

"California," I said. "Los Angeles."

I'd answered well, and Ronnie beamed. He released a salvo of coast versus coast jokes and then launched into a lounge lizard arrangement of "I Love L.A."

"Isn't he great?" asked our tan neighbor when he was done. And he was great, a truly wondrous marriage of talent and technology. He could even be a deejay without standing in a booth. Just by pushing buttons on a little box attached to his keyboard, he could cue up CDs and insert sound effects. Ronnie gave utterly new meaning to the concept of 'one-man band.'

We stayed for hours in the Tiki bar, chatting with our neighbors and listening to Ronnie's endless repertoire. Ray and Pat, our tan neighbors in the flip-flops, were full of hurricane tales and alligator yarns, and Ray was dead right. Ronnie was fantastic.

All of which goes to show. Retirement resorts and Tiki bars and mechanized musicians may not be my carrot or my cup of tea, but what does it matter whose favorite treat they are, whose beverage of choice? There's an ancient rule that's been known to travelers since Odysseus plied the waves. If a new dish is put in front of you, taste it. You don't have to get the recipe, and you aren't even required to clean your plate. Just open your trap a little, let somebody else's ambrosia slip by your epiglottis. Sure there's a risk. You might choke, puke, go into anaphylactic shock. Chances are, though, you won't. Chances are you'll end up pinching yourself. You won't be able to believe it's really a wide-awake you enjoying another Mai Tai at a Tiki bar with Ronnie on the virtual ukelele.

· 14 ·

Run for the Roses

The Belly Button of Uncle Sam

The half-submerged tip of Florida exceeded our expectations with regard to flora and fauna, and Key West was hypnotic in its balmy gardens, azure waters, and Mañanaland culture. Mark twisted his knee just after we arrived, and we both got drunk to kill the pain. After we reeled back to the Phoenix from the waterfront bar that had seduced us with "Triples for the Price of Singles!!" I decided to use the Iguana at a pay phone to file a story and collect e-mail. I staggered over to the booth trailing cables and cords, only to find that someone had relieved the thing of its receiver, leaving only naked wires. Our cellular telephone didn't work in the Conch Republic, either, which meant we were even more disconnected than we'd been in Big Bend, Texas.

"Tomorrow will be soon enough," I said to Mark when I'd made it back to the Phoenix with my assorted hardware. "I have another day before I have to admit defeat and use a fax machine."

Under the pall of hangovers, we headed back up Highway 1 the next day and cut across the mainland to Naples on a road that hugs the Tamiami Canal. Somewhere along the way, we noticed we were back under the cellular umbrella that ends shy of uncivilized border zones. There on an earthen berm overlooking the canal, I filed my story under the gaze of two unblinking alligators.

We left Florida through her panhandle, and our wheels kept turning across the continent. Pages flew off the calendar as quickly as the miles disappeared behind the Phoenix. Life in motion was at last routine. At last we had the new life the wildfire had offered by taking all our worldly goods. Bidding farewell to physical encumbrances had been the easy part. The real test had lain in tearing down the mental constructs that had attracted our physical reality in the first place. Building new lives in our minds and furnishing our souls afresh had been a far greater challenge than the surface showed. Like a still pond in the Everglades, much to be reckoned with had lurked beneath the surface.

We slid along in our newly familiar groove, spending a summer in America's big warm paunch, the Midwest. We watched fireworks on the Fourth of July through St. Louis' Gateway Arch, a grand spectacle launched from barges in the Mississippi. As I sat there on the damp grass, looking out over the mighty continent-bisecting river, I felt as though I was sitting in the epicenter of America, the point from which all gringo ripples emanated, the belly button of Uncle Sam.

And that arch. In my California smugness, I had always thought it must be a silly thing, a sorry man-made attempt to compete with Yosemite, a manufactured tourist attraction built to break the monotonous flatness of a riparian plain.

But photographs and key chain replicas are masters of deception. I was utterly unprepared for the simple, breath-taking elegance of this monumental masterpiece. It stood gleaming in the sunset, its polished surface now white, now purple, now orange. Its very presence seemed to defy rationality. What creative spirit had first envisioned that huge parabola, and how had that dream ignited others until it took shape in three-dimensional stainless steel, meeting so impossibly at its 630-foot apex? A dream like that is the human equivalent of a huge glacier, slowing carving its way through granite until Yosemite Valley appears.

It was like our new life, which suddenly, after months of freeform anarchy, had gelled into something with an identifiable presence, a routine, a philosophy, a norm. Gradually the chaos that we sometimes mistake for freedom had organized itself into a lifestyle. Ironically, we felt freer now that a semblance of order had given structure to our journey.

Extreme Pageantry

At the end of 1995, we returned to Pasadena, not because it was our home, but because it was the home of that New Year's staple, the Rose Parade. Mark had joined the force of white suited volunteers that mobilizes the parade nearly ten years before, and after a year's leave of absence, he wanted to take on a committee assignment again.

There's an old joke that goes like this: A camel is a horse designed by a committee. Well, the Rose Parade is an event designed by 33 committees, and for decades, they've been pulling it off with a remarkable lack of spitting and kicking. It's no mean feat to ensure that sixty floats, each as long as 75 feet, as tall as 60, and weighing as much as 40 tons navigate a five-and-a-half mile route without stalling, crashing into the crowd, or bumping into low bridges. And the floats are only half the story. Twenty-two bands from around the world join the throng, along with 300 horses and riders, and the whole extravaganza is followed by one of the most famous football games in the world. It's easy to be impressed that an event with such a prodigious profile is run by volunteers, and that, in addition to paying for all the costs it incurs, it generates $100 million in business in the Pasadena area every year, and gives $1 million to the city itself.

Mark was eager to be back because he's a born logistician. Nothing delights him more than the complex managerial challenges afforded by extreme pageantry. In years past, he had, among a wide variety of other assignments, shepherded individual floats from design to 'roll-out,' served an ocean of coffee and an Everest of donuts to out-of-town visitors, and driven a truck carrying a portable toilet to volunteers manning street barricades on New Year's Eve.

This year, Mark was one of two "White Suiters" charged with running a temporary city that began to take shape in one of the Rose Bowl's parking lots shortly after Thanksgiving. Its centerpiece was an enormous tent which was unique in possessing no interior upright poles. Supported by a series of metal spans, the thing was big enough to hold a dozen mammoth parade floats and all the people, scaffolding, and paraphernalia required for final decoration. Day by day, equipment and activity increased until, by December 29, the place was the teeming home of 1600 people.

Mark's title was "Barn Chief," and his job amounted to being the enlightened despot of four competing float building firms, one university, scores of employees, hundreds of volunteers, cadres of sponsoring VIPs, visiting Rose princesses, float judges, media entourages, food vendors, souvenir hawkers, and the general public. They needed water, toilets, telephones, electricity, food, lights and heat. The builders needed space to park refrigerated trucks full of flowers, and tents in which they could sort and prepare them for the floats.

The rule that has created the need for extreme measures in the decorating arena is that every superficial inch of every float must be covered with real flowers or other natural vegetative material. It can be shredded, dried, or cut, but it can't be dyed. In their search for a full spectrum of natural colors and textures, float designers scour the world for exotic petals, leaves, bark, seeds, fruits and vegetables. Their ingenuity is boundless, and nothing is too expensive or too mundane to consider as long as it meets the requirement of being natural. A black surface is often achieved with onion seed, and an orange one with dried lentils. Halved limes become bumps on a dinosaur's back, whole potatoes serve as cobblestones, and a metallic look emerges with the smooth application of silvery eucalyptus leaves.

But millions of fresh flowers rule the day, and it's their short shelf life that makes the Rose Parade not only an ephemeral wonder, but also a logistical miracle. Seven million flowers converge on Pasadena from all over the world in those few short days at the end of December, nearly a million-and-a-half roses, and over two million exotics. Chrysanthemums are the most heavily used bloom. Not only are they bright, long-lasting and cheap, they stick well. While fragile flowers must be housed in individual vials of water, mums are sturdy enough to be glued directly onto the plastic-coated metal frameworks of the floats.

Did I say cheap? It's all relative, of course. Fresh flowers are luxury items, and there is nothing cheap about a Rose Parade float. Even the most modest small town entries, the ones built by volunteers and paid for by a year's worth of raffles and pancake breakfasts, cost $75,000. The ones financed by major companies like Kodak and Microsoft can cost four times that much.

And even the most expensive floats end up getting their flowers applied by volunteers. In the last hectic days before "roll-out," thousands of hands are needed. The professional float builders amass those hands by making donations to charitable organizations. The organizations, in return, supply free labor between Christmas and New Year's. They arrive in small armies at the decorating arenas, of which the big tent at the Rose Bowl was only one. Floats are stashed all over Pasadena and the surrounding communities, and each one is a beehive of round-the-clock activity.

Having grown up in Rose Parade country, I'd been a member of a beehive many a year, covering floats in flowers and myself in glue. It was a traditional feature of winter vacation, something to look forward to after the excitement of Christmas. This year, however, I was getting the queen's eye view. Parked inside the enclave at the Rose Bowl, between the mammoth tent and three refrigerated trucks, the Phoenix was at the nerve center of a grand spectacle, and I was living inside it. My only responsibility was to look, marvel, and take Marvin for walks. He was privileged, too. He was the only animal allowed inside the compound.

I watched as Brookside Pavilion began to hum with activity the day after Christmas, and as the hum grew to a roar as New Year's Day approached. I sat in the eye as the hurricane swirled around me. It was exhilarating, energizing, hilarious. It united people in the shared anticipation of an inexorable deadline, and it had all the excitement of a natural disaster without any death or destruction. Best of all, it smelled wonderful. For a week, I lived in a bower, surrounded by the scent of a million roses.

Virtual Guinea Pigs

As I walked among the giant floral sculptures and watched the labor of a thousand hands emerge, I let my mind wander back to the beginning of our journey. Pasadena was no longer our home, but once it had been. Spiraling back to where our adventure had started gave me the chance to pause, assess, consider. It made me look back and forward and around. As 1995 came to a close, as I wondered where our travels might take us next, I thought again about the revolution in electronic communication.

It had been nearly two years since I first slid an America Online disk into the side of my laptop, and eighteen months since I'd first awakened the black box and succeeded in sending e-mail on the fly. I'd driven from peak to peak in the Rockies in search of a cellular signal, and I'd cajoled the Iguana into boondocking with alien pay phones in border zones. I'd read a ream of press releases, scoured a thousand magazines in search of better answers, but the only improvement in my situation had come in the cellular arena. Cell sites had multiplied across the continent, and the likelihood that our telephone would work at a given time and place had increased. Other than that, things hadn't changed since that momentous day in Susanville when I first coaxed the black box to speak. The explosions were all happening on another front. Across the continent, e-mail and America Online were catching on faster than hula hoops.

Back in March, 1994, when I first established my address in cyberspace, I immediately sent messages to the handful of friends who had preceded me there. Two were college professors, and another worked for a computer company. E-mail came with their jobs. I had only one friend who could send and receive e-mail at home, and I was the only person I knew who had it to make a mobile lifestyle possible. Over the next eighteen months, the most common e-mail message Mark and I received went something like this:

"HI. JUST GOT EMAIL AND THIS IS FIRST ATTEMPT TO SEND MESSAGE. DON'T KNOW IF THIS WILL WORK BUT WILL TRY. OVER AND OUT."

One of the reasons that we were the lucky recipients of so many virgin e-mail missives is that we'd been writing and sending a newsletter every month since we'd hit the road. Staying in touch was high on our list of priorities, and we knew we'd never send enough post cards to bridge the gap. The *Phoenix One Journal* went out every month with our e-mail address printed in the masthead, and as our friends and families joined us in cyber-space, it was a handy target for their virtual guinea pigs.

When we left town, the *Phoenix One Journal*'s mailing list had just under a hundred names on it. Each month, Mark and I would tap out stories for it on our laptop computer, and I would pummel our musings into a format we could photocopy on two sides of a sheet of white paper. We included a picture or two, which meant we'd have to seek out a print shop with the machinery required to convert a photograph into a format that a Xerox machine could reproduce.

It usually took us a week to complete the whole process, from writing to licking the stamps, mostly because we were always in new territory, always having to ask, "Where's the post office?" or "Where can we buy a new printer cartridge?" If you want to run an office on the road, you have to allow extra time.

The mailing list for the *Phoenix One Journal* grew as we traveled, and so did our electronic address book. Not long before we arrived at the Rose Bowl at the end of 1995, we began to get e-mail messages akin to this one:

"Have you ever thought about sending your newsletter by e-mail? It would save you a lot on postage," and "It's easy to visualize your newsletter on a home page."

Home page. I'd heard the term. Since I was still limited in my access to the World Wide Web by my tenuous and slow cellular connection and my membership in the not-quite-the-Internet club of America Online, I wasn't sure exactly how it worked. What I grasped immediately was that if you put something on a home page, anyone in the whole wide world with Internet access could look at it. "It's perfect for us," I said to Mark. "We should put our newsletter on the Internet."

But Mark was unimpressed. "I just don't like it," he said. "Not very many people look at home pages, and our mailing list is full of people who probably never will."

While Rose Parade 1996 took shape around me, while I lived in the vortex of that splendid floral storm, I made use of another privilege that came with our exclusive address. There at the Rose Bowl, the Phoenix One had real phone service. In the shadow of the big tent, I wiggled through the AOL wormhole to the World Wide Web. By the time the floats rolled out to meet the new year, I was ready to roll, too, on a whole new highway. Once again, I'd have to sell Mark on the concept, but the World Wide Web was calling me to a new adventure. No longer would e-mail on the fly be enough. If I was really going to live and work on the road, I needed to stake a claim in cyberspace.

Road Trip To Cyberspace

There are two long-standing traditions that govern the Rose Parade. A million people attend, and it never rains. If you move to Pasadena, remember these two legends and state them frequently, with authority. You'll immediately be mistaken for someone who grew up spending New Year's Eve in a sleeping bag on Colorado Boulevard.

But you better know a few other things about Pasadena, too, because on the 364 parade-free days of the year, other things come up besides roses. It's the home of the California Institute of Technology and its famous offspring, the Jet Propulsion Laboratory. It's got the Planetary Society, Art Center College of Design, and several large engineering firms with global reputations. What all of this means is that a lot of creative nerds call Pasadena home.

Because Pasadena is the ancestral stomping ground of such a prodigious number of engineers, graphic designers, scientists, and intellectuals, it's not surprising that it became an Internet boomtown early on in the Web rush. After the last parade float went back into hibernation and 1996 was officially launched, we began to notice how quickly our old home town was launching itself into cyberspace.

Web rush fever was epidemic in Pasadena at the beginning of 1996. It seemed as though everyone had either caught it or was looking for a vaccination, but nobody could avoid the subject. I was eager to join the fray, and Mark had changed his tune since I'd first suggested the idea of publishing the *Phoenix One Journal* on the Internet. He still didn't think posting our newsletter was a great idea, but the Internet seemed to offer some other seductive possibilities. We might resurrect our retail business online, we thought, and sell games, toys, and crafts from across the continent. E-mail had given us the ability to stay connected while we roamed. Virtual commerce dovetailed perfectly with our expanded dreams of totally connected mobility.

By the end of January, we'd metamorphosed into latter-day Jayhawkers, emulating our antecedents who'd planned and schemed for months before heading west with the Gold Rush. Like them, we knew we'd need equipment for our journey, and we paid a visit to Wes Ferrari, whose expertise in the hardware arena had been invaluable in outfitting the Phoenix One two years before.

As we had expected, Wes was a tsunami of information about the latest developments in laptops, modems, and networks. He recommended a company in Los Angeles that hosted Web sites, and Mark called one Friday morning to set a time to visit. "We have an appointment for Tuesday afternoon," he said as he hung up. "So you have until then to think of all your questions."

But actually, I had no time at all. Serendipity intervened in the forms of Bill and Melissa Paule, whom we met unexpectedly the very next day. Melissa and Bill had founded Intelligent Information Innovations less than a year before, a company that offered Website design and hosting. Based in Pasadena, their major clients were companies that made components for cars and motorcycles, and they had just launched an instantly popular site promoting Heidi Wear, a line of clothing marketed by Heidi Fleiss, the "Hollywood Madam."

We canceled our Tuesday meeting and met Bill and Melissa in their offices in Old Pasadena on Monday. Before the afternoon was out, a partnership had begun to blossom. Intelligent Information Innovations needed salespeople to market its web design and hosting services, and we were looking for something to sell as we traveled. Bill and Melissa were as eager as we were to stake new claims in the virtual universe, to design Web sites that could generate income.

The theory was, in those early Web rush days, that a Web site was a hybrid of television and print. Advertisers would be eager to place banners on sites with large audiences, and the price tags would be commensurate with what their counterparts cost in other media. "Content is king," was the ubiquitous catch phrase, because content would lure surfers whose eyeballs could be counted and used to sell ads.

It was a playing field the likes of which the world had never seen. Unlike television, you didn't have to own prohibitively expensive machinery and obtain governmental permission to exploit the medium. Unlike print, you didn't have to invest huge sums in paper and ink and distribution. The Web brought publishing at a global level into the reach of ordinary mortals, anyone who had access to computers and the willingness to learn some idiosyncratic codes. The field was as level as such arenas ever get, the perfect turf for entrepreneurs with grand dreams.

Within a week, Bill, Melissa, Mark and I had decided on two courses of action. Mark and I would create marketing materials for Intelligent Information Innovations and sell Web sites and services on commission. The other project was a magazine-style Web site for which we would build an audience and sell advertising. Bill and Melissa would provide technical expertise and support. Mark and I would provide the content. The site would be a virtual version of our travels, with daily updates 'posted from the road.'

After several brainstorming sessions and multiple electronic queries to the agency that oversees the naming of virtual domains, we decided to call the enterprise *RoadTrip America*. On February 14, 1996, we gathered at the offices of Intelligent Information Innovations. After Bill performed the necessary computer wizardry to bring "www.RoadTripAmerica.com" to life, we drank champagne, ate chocolate cake, and felt very proud. The world was our oyster, and we were sitting on top of it. We were Jayhawkers, and we'd just joined the rush to the virtual gold fields.

The excitement didn't wear off as we plunged into the endless process of designing and furnishing our new domain, an undertaking that began with hardware. Back we went to Wes Ferrari, who procured for us a new, more powerful laptop and a new, more powerful modem. He also helped us choose a device with which the world was only beginning to become acquainted, a digital camera. Armed with the machine to write and edit, the machine to transmit data, and the machine to trap images in digitized format, we were forty-niners with wagon, horse and shovel. We were ready to roll.

Well, almost. I had a heck of a lot to learn, and if *RoadTrip America* was going to be the wonderful Internet oasis we'd envisioned, it was going to take a lot of hours to build it. As anyone who has ever constructed a virtual development knows, it takes as much planning, design, engineering, and plain old brick-laying as anything in the realm of three dimensions. Don't be fooled by the lack of cement mixers. Building empires on the World Wide Web may be done by troglodytes with soft bellies and carpal tunnel syndrome, but it's hard labor nonetheless.

The four of us undertook it with the enthusiasm that only real trail blazing ignites. I spent endless days delving into the intricacies of Adobe Photoshop, and endless nights immersed in HTML code. If my learning curve were to appear in three dimensions, it would rival the Gateway Arch in angle and height, but somehow it was all challenge and no chore. We were creating something exciting and new, scaling the world's latest Everest. We were making measurable progress in our quest for a life on the road and a business that would keep abreast.

We kept thinking we were almost done, but it was nearly six weeks later that a full-fledged *RoadTrip America* appeared on the World Wide Web. It had a home page upon which a new feature would appear every day, and, in addition to pages for Mark, Marvin, the Phoenix One and me, it had eleven other departments for funny road signs, stories about people, places, restaurants, animals, and unusual vehicles, slide shows, a post office, a game, and every single one of the *Phoenix One Journals*. At the post office, visitors could "send" an electronic postcard to anybody with an e-mail address. The game, called "What IS That Thing?" had pictures of obscure objects whose identity viewers could guess by clicking on possible answers.

The basic concept was that every day we'd post a new feature on the home page, and then "retire" it to its corresponding department, where it would reside indefinitely. Each department had its own directory, and Bill also installed a search program that could locate any word in the site. We wanted people to visit *RoadTrip America* every day as vicarious travelers, but since the number of features would be growing at a fast clip, we wanted people to be able to sift through everything as easily as possible.

The Phoenix One section was designed to attract sponsors. Melissa designed pages that allowed viewers to take a virtual

tour both inside and out. With the digital camera, we pho-
tographed every major component from air conditioner to water
heater and wrote descriptive articles for each. For the inside tour,
we included pictures and descriptions of all our mobile office
equipment. Every manufacturer became a potential advertiser.

Suddenly, our course of action for the rest of 1996 was
mapped. Unlike the previous two years, where we'd taken for
granted the luxury of moseying, we were journalists and salespeople now. Not only did we have to find and write a feature
every day, we had to call prospective sponsors, clients and
advertisers. We'd been asking for a business we could travel
with, and now we had it in spades.

Stealth Journalism

One of the first events we covered as *RoadTrip America* was
the "Muroc Reunion,"a car race in the Mojave Desert on Rogers
Dry Lake, which lies within the boundaries of Edwards Air Force
Base. It was a reunion because back in the twenties, car buffs
used to gather at the lake to race where they didn't have to abide
by speed limits. When the Air Force decided to use the lake as a
runway, the rallies came to an end. In 1996, the Air Force gave
permission for a nostalgic reunion, as long as attendees didn't
bring any alcohol, leave any trash, or take pictures of the Stealth
bomber parked nearby. We found out about it from Bob Hyde,
who worked at a place where we bought propane. His friends
owned a souped-up roadster called "Dad's Dream." "I'll be in
the crew," said Bob. "I can introduce you to everyone else."

It was the perfect maiden voyage for a couple of newly-
hatched Web journalists, and the perfect event to inaugurate our
"Wheels" department. I'd never been to a dry lake before, and I
saw immediately why they're popular with pilots and racers.
Mirror flat and rock hard, it stretched for miles, ending at bare
hills on the horizon. The surface was white, the sky was blue,
and the whole effect was distinctly other-worldly. We joined a
row of other motor homes along one edge of what would become
the raceway and went in search of Bob Hyde and "Dad's Dream."

We walked to the end of the row of motorhomes, where a
bivouac of tents covered commercial displays and classic cars of

bygone eras. From there we made our way to "pit row," where crew after crew were readying their vehicles for the next trials. The race was open to anything with wheels, and entries included motorcycles, antique trucks, old hot rods, slick new "Streamliners," beefed up dune buggies, and anything else whose mettle the owner wanted to test. Amid this array of automotive oomph, we came upon three men standing next to what I can only describe as a rocket car. One of the men was wearing a white cowboy hat.

Mark and I, new as we were to journalism, were a bit hesitant about walking up and sticking our notebooks and camera into strange faces, but the man in the cowboy hat helped us out.

"What kind of camera is that?" he asked as we paused to admire his car. I showed him the digital camera and explained how it didn't use film. "Well, take a picture of 'Danny Boy,' here," he said, pointing to the rocket car. "'Danny Boy' set the D-Gas record of 315 miles an hour."

The ice was broken, and soon we were asking questions, taking notes, and explaining how to look at *RoadTrip America* on the World Wide Web. Ed Tradup, the man in the cowboy hat, told us how he and his friend Richard Thomason were apple farmers from Brewster, Washington. Ed was a drag racer, and Richard raced motorcycles. When Ed told Richard he wanted to belong to the "200 mph club," Richard had replied, "There's no respect for 200. Let's go for 300." In 1991, they exceeded their goal at the Bonneville Salt Flats in Utah.

Before we left, Ed shook our hands, gave us each an apple and said, "Just remember, everybody here wants to talk about their cars. You don't have to be shy about asking."

Ed was right. Everybody did want to talk, and, with few exceptions, everybody's been talking to us ever since. I can't say it's always easy to approach a stranger and start asking questions, but when your goal is not to embarrass or expose, but to share and showcase, just about everybody warms to the occasion.

Marvin wasn't quite as thrilled by our shakedown cruise to Muroc. There wasn't a bush or a blade of grass for miles, and I had the feeling that the flat, hard surface of the lake bed seemed like a floor to him, an indoor surface, a surface upon which he was unable to lift a leg. I took him for a long walk, but nothing I could say would convince him that things weren't going to change, and that if he didn't bite the bullet and pee anyway, he'd have a very long weekend. We returned, and Mark said he'd have a try. "I saw a bush over near the hangar where the Stealth bomber is parked," he said. "We'll aim for that."

Half an hour later, they were back at the Phoenix, and Marvin was still wearing a pained look. "We got within fifteen feet," Mark said, "When a soldier with a machine gun appeared and said, 'I'm sorry sir, but you can't take another step closer.' I explained how Marvin really needed that bush, but he said, 'Sorry. Back off.'" Marvin was finally able to relieve himself after dark against the side of a portable toilet.

The next day, the wind, which had been utterly absent when we arrived, kicked up a storm. Racing had to be suspended as little dust devils and tiny funnel clouds darted over the lake and coated everything in fine white dust. Fearing what the stuff might do to my laptop, I kept the Phoenix shut up tight. Even so, it took weeks before the last of Muroc was removed from all the nooks and crannies.

The Muroc Reunion was a complete success, and a true test of whether *RoadTrip America* was really going to work. I'd sent stories and images by cellular connection to Melissa, who posted them to the Web. Our equipment had weathered adverse conditions without ceasing to function, and Mark and I had metamorphosed into cub reporters. Even the Road Dog had passed an endurance test and proved he could go the distance. We'd already learned how to live on the road. Now it looked as though we could work there full time, too. We could even have Charles Kuralt's job without working for CBS. The world was indeed our oyster.

· 15 ·

On the Road and Online

Buffalo Shadow

Our first personal interview as Internet journalists took us to Jacumba, a small town just north of the Mexican border in the desert east of San Diego. We had an appointment to talk to an old-timer, a prospector named Don Weaver who had scoured the hills for decades in search of tourmaline and gold.

Our directions were the kind that took us off the map on a dirt road and included large objects as landmarks: "Go past the pile of rocks," and "Fork left at the big cactus." With little effort, we were soon lost in the border zone, and it wasn't long before we arrived at a landmark that caught us wholly by surprise.

It was a huge wall built of steel girders and concrete pilings. Topped with a thorned crown of razor wire, it was clearly a project with no less a goal than to form an impassable barrier between the United States and Mexico. I hadn't seen anything like it since I visited East Germany in the seventies.

"I can't believe it," I said as we came to a halt in front of the forbidding structure. "I can't believe this exists in the same country that spent so much time talking about how awful the Berlin Wall was." But there it was, and the only difference was that this unsightly edifice, probably because of its isolated location, had managed to avoid the nightly news.

We turned around in a clearing in front of the wall and headed back the way we came. A hundred yards back up the road, three men had emerged from a house to take a look at our alien vehicle. We stopped, and Mark asked for directions. All three knew where Don Weaver lived, and, armed with a new set of landmarks, we set out afresh.

This time, we reached our destination without detour, and a gray-haired lady in a flowered blouse came outside to greet us.

"I'm Grace Helen," she said. "Come on up."

We followed her up several stone steps to a patio covered by a blooming bougainvillea vine.

"Don will be right out," said Grace Helen. "Please sit down."

We sat, and soon Don appeared, hobbling painfully on a cane.

"Hello," he said gruffly. "If I'd known how to reach you, I would have told you not to come."

Taken aback, I said, "If this isn't a good time, we can leave."

"No, no, you're here," said Don as he lowered himself into a folding chair. "It's just that I slipped yesterday and landed on my hip, and I'm just not doing very well. But you're here, so tell me what you want to know."

This was our first serious interview, the first time we'd called someone up, identified ourselves as being with *RoadTrip America*, a feature magazine on the World Wide Web." We didn't find ourselves speechless, but we were hardly seasoned. Since Don Weaver was a prospector, it seemed only reasonable to start out asking questions about rocks and mines and ore.

It didn't take long before our conversation had gone beyond pegmatite dykes and quartz outcroppings. As Don relaxed into story-telling mode and realized his audience was genuinely interested, he told us about a rock crushing mill he built in 1951 at a place over the border called Dos Cabezas. He used the now-defunct San Diego & Imperial Valley Railroad to ship white limestone to roofers in Southern California. The railroad had been completed in 1919 at enormous expense by the

Spreckels sugar dynasty over terrain so treacherous it was called the "impossible track." It took 16 major tunnels and 21 trestles to complete the run from Mexico to California, and the wooden span over Goat Canyon still holds the world record for length and height.

"It wasn't easy to use that railroad, but it was too hot to use trucks, and the road was too bad," Don said. "It was hard to keep workers, too," he added. To make things a little easier, he invented and built a portable mill that he could move from location to location.

Don went on to tell us about other businesses he'd owned and prospecting he'd done all over the Southwest. He told us how he'd discovered gold in Arizona, and sold a lucrative option on his claim. "They never did anything with it, though," he said. "The gold's still there. I could take you right to it."

By this time, we were all feeling more comfortable, and I asked Don about his childhood. His eyes immediately took on a faraway look.

"I was born on the Cimarron River in a plum thicket," said Don. "Renegades were chasing my parents. After my mother had me, my father said, 'Leave that little spotted pony for Don. He'll catch up with us.'"

The story progressed, and before our eyes Don Weaver, the prospector, disappeared. In his place, a new personage emerged, a regal, powerful one. Where just a few minutes before an ancient prospector had sat crippled in pain, we found ourselves gazing upon Buffalo Shadow, the Delaware Indian chief. Suddenly he rose, and with vigor he hadn't possessed when we arrived, he disappeared into the house.

In a few minutes, he returned with two long wooden cases. He opened the first and removed a long peace pipe carved from smooth dark wood. "This is my chief's pipe," he said, "My calumet." As we admired its exquisite craftsmanship, Buffalo Shadow opened the other case. "And this is my jewelry," he said, holding up a heavy necklace made of carved bone, beads and polished stones.

"Can you put it on?" I blurted. I looked at Mark nervously. Was that a rude thing to ask?

But Buffalo Shadow didn't seem to mind. He fastened the heavy necklace around his throat and sat down.

"My nephew made this calumet out of rare native woods," he said. "It's the only one of its kind in the world."

The conversation flowed now, and suddenly we realized we had been transfixed for three hours. "We must go," Mark said at last. "You need to rest, and we've taken too much of your day."

"Wait," said Buffalo Shadow rising, and once again he disappeared into the house. He returned carrying another calumet in his hands, a beautiful thing made of light wood and decorated with beads and feathers.

"This is for you," he said simply, and our protests went unheeded. "I'm glad you came," said Buffalo Shadow as he placed the calumet in Mark's hands. "Have a good, safe journey, and perhaps our paths will cross again someday."

We were both silent as we drove away. When we reached the highway and headed east, Mark said, "Did you notice how his voice changed when he wasn't Don Weaver any more, but Buffalo Shadow?"

"He wasn't sick any more, either," I said. "When he put the necklace on, it seemed to clothe him in youth and strength."

We were quiet again as we crossed California on Interstate 8. Our day had been such a surprise, such a memorable initiation into our new role as journalists. Watching Don Weaver metamorphose into Buffalo Shadow reminded us that people and places are never one-dimensional, that everyone has a story under the surface, a role beyond the visible mask.

A few days later, Buffalo Shadow astonished us once more by proving that, properly motivated, just about anybody could find a window to the World Wide Web, even in 1996, even if they were eighty-one years old, knew nothing about computers, and lived off the map.

When we left, we'd promised to send the chief a print version of the story we would write for *RoadTrip America*. It wasn't something we wanted to form a habit of doing, but the Web was still new to many people, and we were afraid that Buffalo Shadow might never see his story otherwise. Jacumba was isolated, after all, not the sort of place you'd expect to find the latest in communications technology.

Before we had a chance to print and mail a copy of the story, we received a telephone message. Buffalo Shadow had seen the story online, he said, and thank you. And thanks for coming, and safe journey.

"Looks like Buffalo Shadow caught up with us," said Mark, "And we didn't even leave him a spotted pony."

You Can't Tell A Cybernaut By His Coveralls

The week after the story appeared on *RoadTrip America*, we received an appreciative e-mail message from the chief's niece in Colorado. We had an invitation to visit a nephew who lived on the Olympic Peninsula in a bear preserve, and another to meet the artist in Tucson who made our calumet. Not only did this unexpected and farflung response reinforce our belief that the interactivity of the World Wide Web imbued it with connective powers we had yet to fully appreciate, it shattered an assumption I'd hit the road with.

Without giving the subject second thought, I had assumed that people in isolated places would be the last to find connection to the Internet. Buffalo Shadow was my first inkling that the opposite might be true. Just as you're more likely to find an airplane parked next to a cabin in Alaska than beside a suburban split level in Chicago, I soon learned that the appeal of electronic communication was stronger in the boondocks than it was in Manhattan.

Before we left Pasadena as *RoadTrip America*, we'd emblazoned the Phoenix One with new graphics heralding our Internet presence. On both sides, we included that mysterious and cutting edge code, our address on the World Wide Web. For most of 1996, we never saw another URL on a vehicle, and ours attracted attention wherever we went. It's the primary way we learned never to predict who was wired and who wasn't. In those days, a power dresser with a cell phone could easily be an Internet illiterate, and a rube in a straw hat might be a cyber pro.

We pulled into a campground north of Seattle one afternoon and parked across from an old trailer with rotting wheels. A man of indeterminate age and weathered countenance emerged to look us over. He was wearing a torn shirt and faded denim overalls, and he had a large bottle of malt liquor in his hand. He sized us up for a few silent minutes and then vanished inside.

An hour later, we went outside to take Marvin for a walk. When we returned, our neighbor greeted us.

"I took a look at y'all's Web site," he said, "And I liked it. I specially liked y'all's game. I guessed mosta them gizmos right on my first try."

"Uh, thanks," I said, suppressing the urge to let my mouth drop open. We introduced ourselves and spent an hour or so with Will, swapping computing tips and even some recipes.

"My favorite drink is Guinness and espresso coffee, mixed half-and-half," he said. "A big ol' glass o' that and yer buzzed and wide-awake at the same time." I haven't found the right occasion to try the drink yet, but Will convinced me on the spot that I risked serious offense if I relied on preconceived notions to identify Web surfers. He proved beyond a doubt that you couldn't tell a cybernaut by his coveralls.

Even armed with this knowledge, we risked offense at every turn. In Arizona, shortly after our meeting with Buffalo Shadow, Mark went into the public library in a little town called Ajo. We had printed postcards announcing RoadTrip America's debut, and libraries were beginning to install Web browsers.

"I might as well let them know about us," Mark said, and I took Marvin for a stroll around the town center while he went inside.

He was back before we'd covered two sides of the square.

"Brother," he said. "I'm lucky I got out without being arrested."

"What happened?" I asked. "Did you talk too loud?"

"All I did was go up to the counter and ask to talk to the librarian. I showed her the card and explained that we were currently posting stories about Arizona. I said that if the library had a Web browser, her patrons might find our site interesting.

"I might as well have offered her cocaine. 'Oh, no!' she exclaimed. 'No, no, no! We can't do anything like that without approval from Phoenix.' She wouldn't even let me leave the card on the counter, and as I left, I heard her making a phone call. For all I know, the library gestapo may soon be on my tail."

I would be willing to wager serious money that the same

little library has at least one Web browser now, and it may well have half a dozen. The same librarian is probably teaching someone how to surf as I write this. Free Web access has become nearly universal in public libraries across the land. Libraries are the gateways to cyberspace for persons of limited means or experience, and since they often have fast connections, plenty of experienced Web surfers take advantage of them, too.

But things were different in May, 1996, and we could never be sure how Internet journalists would be received. We played it safe. We kept our self-introductions short, neutral, and polite, and if we came face to face with technophobes, we beat a diplomatic retreat. It was our view that a medium of such power would ultimately win no matter what stance we took, and we were happier as ambassadors than foot soldiers.

"For the Glory!"

Online, however, we were preaching to the converted. As search engines and directories began discovering *RoadTrip America* and announcing it as a "site of the day" or "pick of the week," we began to develop a friendly following. One day, while we were still in southern Arizona, we received this message:

> I'm new to your site, but if you are looking for a real adventure and you are in California over Memorial Day Weekend, you should head up to Eureka and see the Kinetic Sculpture Race. About fifty grown-up people create sculptures that they race cross-country for the three days. They have to be human powered and must cross obstacles like the Eel River, Humboldt Bay, sand dunes, mud flats, etc., etc. Awards are given for speed but also for art and engineering. Some sculptures are powered by six or eight people.
>
> It's worth a detour.
> Ellen

Memorial Day was hard upon us, and Eureka, California, was over a thousand miles away. On the other hand, the glory of interactivity had brought us an enticing tip. We'd said we'd take advice from readers, do what they said, go where they pointed. What was preventing us, after all If it was worth a detour, why not one across two deserts and three mountain ranges?

We couldn't come up with a good reason not to make a run for the north coast, and Ellen kept sending us further seductive tidbits about the Kinetic Sculpture Race, like "There's a prize for the first sculpture to break down," and "Bribing of race officials is condoned — come to think of it, it might even be encouraged."

"Well," said Mark, closing the road atlas, "If we leave tomorrow, we have three days to get there. What do you say?"

"I say we're *RoadTrip America*," I replied. "We owe it to our audience."

The next morning, we headed northwest on a beeline for redwood country.

Our diagonal route from Ajo to Eureka took us over small, little traveled roads, first across the arid expanse of Arizona, and then through sandy windstorms between Las Vegas and Reno. We wound through the Sierras across eastern California and dropped down into the central valley at Redding. Traveling with blinders on, we were trying to ignore the countless vistas, towns, and monuments that would have made ideal subject matter for *RoadTrip America*. Having made up our minds to get to the Kinetic Sculpture Race or break down in the attempt, we focused on our destination. We were counting miles, covering ground.

It was a difficult shift after so many months spent cultivating the art of moseying, and at a rest stop near Redding, we almost slipped off our trajectory. We'd just returned to the Phoenix from taking Marvin for a walk when a man and a woman walked up, curious about the big truck with the URL on the side. When we explained about *RoadTrip America*, they were full of fascinating tidbits about the surrounding area.

"There's a restaurant near here you really ought to check out," the man said. "It was founded by some people who won the lottery a few years back. They started a bunch of businesses in the town with their winnings, but the restaurant is the only one that survived. And actually, I think even that loses money, because you get an awfully good meal for eight bucks. They lay on an absolutely amazing spread."

It was tempting, and I have no doubt that the jackpot restaurant and its founders would have been the first pearl in a string of gems we'll probably never know. We'd learned that lesson back in Gila Bend, where the off-season Christmas tree had led to ostriches, wheat harvesters, and a close call months later at the Canadian border. Stories don't exist in isolation. Every one of them opens a lid on a Pandora's box of unpredictable marvels. Each is a jewel in a strand of people, places, and events that can last as long as the rest of your life.

We were already a few links into the chain that connected us to Humboldt County and the Kinetic Sculpture Race. Not only had we told Ellen we'd be there, we'd already called its founder, an artist named Hobart Brown. We would be welcomed as members of the media, he'd promised. We'd get press passes and more cooperation than we could possibly use.

"We wish we could take your advice right this minute," I said to our roadside tipsters, "But we've got to get to the coast before dark."

"But we'll be back," said Mark. "And thank you."

Will we really return? Who can say? The only time you realize how many wonders are waiting to be discovered is when you have the audacity to try to see them all. North America was getting bigger with every mile we covered, and cyberspace added a whole new infinite dimension.

We left Redding on Highway 299. The road climbed high through the Trinity Alps and down through the redwoods to the coast. We arrived in time to attend a pre-race press conference in a grand old wooden hotel in Eureka.

The first person I saw when we walked into the room was a little man wearing khaki shorts, knee socks, a chest full of military medals, and a fake nose as long as a hot dog. Near him stood three muscular-looking young men with papier maché watermelons on their heads. As I continued looking around the room, my eyes found not a single ordinary soul to rest upon.

"Do you think we're in the right place?" I whispered. There was no overt indication that these were indeed the competitors in Hobart Brown's "Triathlon of Art."

"I don't just think it," said Mark. "I know it."

And of course he was right. We'd found our kinetic sculptors, and soon we discovered their chief. Hobart Brown was a smiling elf wearing black tails and a top hat. He welcomed us warmly and made sure we received our press credentials.

"They'll come in handy at popular viewing locations like

Dead Man's Drop and the Slimy Slope," he said. "You'll be able to stand in good places to take pictures."

As Ellen had suggested and we were beginning to discover, the Kinetic Sculpture race is a many-splendored thing. Not only does it last for three days and cover 42 miles over land and water, it has grown its own culture and elaborate liturgy of traditions. What Hobart Brown had started back in 1969 by challenging one other person to a race in front of his art gallery had grown to attract 137 works of human-powered art, some from as far away as Seattle. According to the official rules, they had all come, not to win prizes, but "For the Glory."

And we covered the whole thing "For the Glory," from the chaotic beginning in Arcata's central square to the finish line in Ferndale. On Saturday, we slogged up a mosquito-infested sand dune to watch, among others, a rolling watermelon and a one-man cheese navigate Dead Man's Drop. We gathered with the crowds on Sunday morning at the boat ramp, and we were as disappointed as anyone when the Coast Guard announced that the water in Humboldt Bay was too rough for crafts of dubious buoyancy. It didn't stop eight stone-thighed Oregonians from pedaling into the water aboard a giant contraption called the "Maltese Fulcrum." The thing worked better on water than land, and they weren't about to let a little wind keep them from demonstrating. A few other rigs took to the waves to prove their pontoons, and after they all returned to land without serious mishap, the race continued on a detour around the bay.

We were in good company in the press areas. A crew from New York was filming a segment for CBS Sunday Morning, Charles Kuralt's old showcase. While we waited for sculptures to appear at the various viewing points, we chatted with Tom and Russell, the cameraman and audio engineer, who were from Los Angeles and thrilled to be covering something besides the O.J. Simpson trial.

"This is like a vacation after all those months on the steps of the L.A. Courthouse," said Russell, and he was right. His producer chartered a helicopter and a water taxi to make sure they got all the best shots.

The Phoenix was stuck on land, but since the sculptures were, too, it didn't make much difference. We followed them over hill and dale, watching as an animated, smoke-exhaling dragon caused a stampede among a herd of dairy cows, and a large ear of corn broke down on a railroad crossing. "For the Glory!" we heard the crew yell as the cob cleared the tracks at last.

By the third day, we'd taken hundreds of pictures, rescued a girl who had fallen head first into the mud hole at the bottom of the Slimy Slope, and made friends with such personages as the newly crowned Quagmire Queen, Lord Ductape, the Rampmeister, and the Official Unofficial Official. We'd also met a compatriot who was taking pictures to post on the race's Web site. Larry Goldberg was the owner of Northcoast Internet, the major Internet service provider in the area. When we told him about *RoadTrip America*, he was eager to hear more and offer support to fellow cyber-reporters.

"You're welcome to use our T-1 connection to surf the Web," he said. "Or just come by and visit our offices after the race sometime."

When the "27th Annual World Championship Great Arcata to Ferndale Cross-Country Kinetic Sculpture Race (The Greatest Race on the Planet)" passed into history, we did indeed find our way to the offices of Northcoast Internet in Eureka. Larry, who was originally from New York, was a roadtripper from way back and a dyed-in-the-wool entrepreneur. He had founded Northcoast Internet and built it into the leading service provider in Humboldt County, but Larry wasn't resting on any laurels. He was already looking ahead, blazing trails in the uncharted zones of digital communication and Internet commerce. We spent the afternoon swapping roadtrip stories, predictions about the price of banner advertising on the World Wide Web, and the future of mobile communication. Somewhere in the proceedings, Larry invited us to dinner at his home near Trinidad. "And you're welcome to stay with us, too, if you like," he said.

Larry's wife Kathleen, after recovering from the shock of having two strangers in a motorhome show up on her doorstep at dinnertime, welcomed us warmly, and the conversation continued far into the night. It was the beginning of an evolving friendship that blossomed by e-mail after we departed and ultimately gave *RoadTrip America* a new home. The Phoenix One can wander at will, but a web site's files have to live in stationary, three-dimensional hardware. In 1997, thanks to Larry Goldberg, *RoadTrip America* took up residence in redwood country.

We met Larry because of Hobart and Hobart because of Ellen, and it all goes to show that you never know how many pearls you'll add to your string when you take the time to follow one suggestion, and how many gems you'll keep on adding as you keep on making tracks. Now that we were traveling two highways at once, making connections in cyberspace as well as on solid ground, our network of friends and acquaintances was growing by quantum leap. On the road and online, what had started as a simple series of connected links was now burgeoning into an ever-expanding blanket of virtual chain mail.

Our online audience was growing steadily, and our sights were still set on selling advertising. We called the manufacturers we'd identified as we developed *RoadTrip America*. The novelty of the Web was an instant ice breaker, and people were eager to talk about the promise of the new medium. When it came to making actual sales, however, nobody wanted to jump in first. If they were willing to test the waters at all, they weren't prepared to pay for the opportunity. There were times when I felt as though I was selling a product on a par with lunar cheese.

After three months of countless conversations and innumerable predictions of what the world was coming to, we had chalked up not one significant sale. Our only solace was that big companies weren't doing any better. We were failing just as successfully as the Boston Globe and Microsoft. Big and little, the Jayhawkers of the World Wide Web were foundering in uncharted territories.

For us, there was no going back. We were out there, for better or worse, for richer or poorer, uphill and down. As tantalizing as any horizon in three dimensions, the virtual frontier still beckoned, still promised wondrous things. Any medium with the power to link us to Ellen and Hobart and Larry by way of Dead Mans's Drop and the Slimy Slope was far too marvelous to dismiss just because our ad space appeared to be worthless. Any good Jayhawker will tell you that gold might have inspired the journey, but getting there was what gave them stories to tell their grandchildren.

Gold Rush fortunes, as successful merchants selling hardware during the Internet revolution will be happy to corroborate, were more likely to be built on peripherals than ingots. Levi Strauss made his pile off denim trousers, and Domingo

Ghirardelli cleaned up with bars of chocolate instead of bullion. Web frenzy helped make Bill Gates the richest man on the planet, and everybody knows it wasn't because he started an online magazine called *Slate*. Just like *RoadTrip America*, *Slate* started losing money as soon as it hit the wires.

So you have to ask. If *Slate* lost money from day one, why was someone like Bill Gates bothering with it? If gold was such a pipe dream, why did Levi Strauss buy stock in mining claims? Why not stick with operating systems and blue jeans and relax at the Ritz? Why bother with rainbows?

The answer is ever the same. The journey's the thing, and as with Hobart's race, you do it "For the Glory." Who's to say whether a trophy awaits you, or whether you'll vanish in a mud hole at the bottom of the Slimy Slope. The only thing you know for sure is that you don't know anything at all until you're eating spaghetti in Ferndale.

We bade farewell to Larry and Kathleen and headed north. *RoadTrip America*'s race had only just begun.

· 16 ·

In League with the Fame Brokers

"THANKS FOR SENDING ME THE WORLD"

In Port Angeles, Washington, the local news anchor, who was also the producer and cameraman, interviewed Mark, Marvin and me for the evening news. A newspaper in California and another in Arizona had run little items about *RoadTrip America*, but this was our television debut. Like the newspaper coverage, the interview caused a small surge in visitors to our Web site when it aired, and it brought us a few more e-mail friends, armchair travelers who told us about places to go and people to meet. We were encouraged by the growth in our audience, and we held firm to the notion that our advertising space would rise in value as our "traffic" increased.

We moseyed about the Olympic Peninsula for a few more days, writing about such attractions as Bandy's Troll Haven, an off-beat resort where castles and dungeons full of trolls are available for rent, and The Three Crabs, a venerable old restaurant on the sand at Dungeness Point. In Seattle, Charlie and Barb Brister, the juggling toymakers, pointed us in the direction of local wonders only natives would know about. First we paid a visit to "Lincoln's Toe Truck," a hot pink rolling pun with a full set of fiberglass piggies on the roof. It sat on a high pedestal in the shadow of the Space Needle, perhaps an eyesore, perhaps a work of art, and definitely a photogenic landmark.

"Don't miss the Boeing Surplus Store," Charlie said, and we headed to Kent to find out what the biggest airplane company in the world was unloading for ten cents on the dollar. The store was a huge warehouse full of shelves, bins, pallets and piles of hardware and office machinery, from the mundane to the mysteriously specialized. In the middle of the cavernous interior, a smiling man welcomed us into his private fiefdom, a room-sized wire cage bearing the sign "World Famous Tool Crib."

"People come here from all over," said Park, who'd been ruling the crib for five years. "We probably stock every swap meet from here to Alaska. A lot of people make a living off what they buy here and resell." I lacked the necessary knowledge to recognize a good price on a self-collating nutplate drill motor or a collapsible mandrel coldwork puller, but I could tell from the glowing faces of other shoppers that the "World Famous Tool Crib" was a candy store for rock hounds, pilots and flea market entrepreneurs. I took a picture of Park holding a drill bit the size of a baseball bat under a cardboard cutout of Bill Boeing, and we continued our tour outside, where a large chain-link pen enclosed the inventory of big stuff: propellers, wheels, restroom units, galleys, and other cast-off portions of jumbo jets. The Boeing Surplus Store was an utterly unique local marvel, another perfect story for *RoadTrip America*.

Thanks to people like Charlie and Barb and our growing legion of vicarious traveling companions, we were never short of story leads. As we had predicted, the interactivity of a Web site gave us two-way connection wherever we traveled, and an immediate letter of introduction to the communities in which we arrived. It may have been easy to dismiss the Internet as a money-losing commercial boondoggle, but it was impossible to ignore its power as a medium of human interaction.

What we were so easily taking for granted with *RoadTrip America* had been science fiction only a few years before. No other medium could have allowed us to announce our location to the world and invite casual, immediate response. Yes, television or radio could have done the announcing, and response by telephone or letter could have been suggested. But it takes courage to make a phone call and time to write a letter. E-mail has the unique capacity to be quick, informal and non-intrusive all at the same time, the perfect ice-breaking medium for messages of introduction and the exchange of ideas. What it all boils down to is this. People who never write letters and would never dream of dialing your telephone number may well send you e-mail. That fact has profound ramifications.

Consider these messages, a few of thousands we've received from the ether. I believe that not a one of them would have reached us by any other medium.

"I think what you are doing is wonderful. I am 68 and this was always my dream and now I can communicate with someone who is living it."

"I'm sitting in a 15 x 7 office with no windows. I'm supposed to be analyzing our computer system, but for the entire day I've been reading your journals. I wish I could do the same as you, and I think I'm going to figure out how. Thanks for the inspiration."

"You are living my dream! I'm a supervisor at the Houston Intercontinental Airport. I'm an Air Traffic Controller. If you swing by here, come up for the royal tour!"

"Yo, Marvin! Greetings to the Cyberdog!" (From the start, Marvin received more e-mail than Mark or me.)

"I'm from Long Island, New York, and I'm 15 years old. I have a couple of questions. How do you receive mail? (Not e-mail, but like bills and stuff) When you rent a movie, do you mail it back? Where do you park at night?"

"THANKS FOR SENDING ME THE WORLD TO TALK TO. IT WAS QUITE A NICE THOUGHT TO DO THAT."

This last message came from a man named Fred Worster, who signed his letters "The MAINEiac Chef." He was bedridden and dependent on oxygen and told us he had "3 TO 8 MONTHS TO LIVE," but "DON'T FEEL BAD FOR ME AS I HAVE HAD A GOOD LIFE."

We struck up an e-mail friendship with Fred. He kept us posted on the view from his window in northern Maine and sent us a recipe for authentic Indian pudding, all in screaming capital letters. In Fred's case, virtual shouting seemed to underscore his desire to make the most of every second of his life, even when a failing heart kept him confined to a hospital bed. Why whisper when you can yell? Why merely exist when you can live?

The inevitable day arrived when an e-mail message appeared in our mailbox from Fred's son Dale.

> "I am sorry to say that my Dad has passed away. He talked about you and your travels. Thanks for being someone in his life."

How do you put a price on the meeting of minds, on friendship and community that transcends physical location, that rises above debilitating illness? As much as I wanted *RoadTrip America*'s ad space to sell, it was almost irrelevant to measure its success in commercial terms.

Almost, but not quite. We had bills to pay, gas tanks to fill. You can't draw checks off your memory bank. We plotted and schemed about ways to build our audience, and one day, I had the bright idea of attending the Calgary Stampede. One of my sisters lives in Calgary, and she'd been telling us for years that Stampede was the rodeo equivalent of the Rose Parade.

Stampede

"It will help build our presence in Canada," I said, "And maybe we can get press credentials." I said "maybe" because we had no way of knowing whether an Internet magazine would be taken seriously. Back then, when Web reporters were unusual, we never knew whether we'd be welcomed as exotic celebrities or scorned as pathetic pretenders.

As it turned out, we were neither pampered nor scorned, but rather welcomed exactly as we'd hoped, on a par with all the other journalists. Most of them had been covering Stampede for years, and all of them wore cowboy hats.

In fact, everyone in Calgary was wearing a cowboy hat, and most were wearing jeans and boots, too. The whole city goes wildly Western for two weeks every July, and if you don't follow the custom, you feel like a Coke at a Pepsi convention.

Before the week was out, we'd made our second television appearance. Mark and I, dutifully wearing newly purchased white straw cowboy hats, were interviewed by a local news crew at the Phoenix One, which was parked near the main Stampede gate. Once again, *RoadTrip America* recorded a surge in visitors, and once again, our e-mailbox was full of complimentary messages and suggestions about places to go and things to see in Alberta.

After Stampede ended, we spent a few days in the hill country north of Calgary, visiting a high-tech dinosaur museum in Drumheller, and interviewing a bull rider and a rodeo clown in Three Hills. As we climbed west over the Canadian Rockies into British Columbia, I watched the staggering scenery roll by and set my mind to work once again on the conundrum of *RoadTrip America*. Were we crazy? Were we brilliant? Were we headed in a direction that made any sense at all, or were we throwing money into the wind?

Sitting in a natural hot pool under the stars at Fairmont, I turned to Mark and said, "If we can create a Web site, so can a hundred thousand other people. Right now, we're unusual, and right now *RoadTrip America* is a story. In six months, we may still be unusual, but I'd be willing to bet that *RoadTrip America* will be yesterday's news. It's too easy to create a Web site, and too many people are doing it."

"Yeah, so what's your point?" asked Mark.

"Well, I've been thinking, and I have an idea," I said, and Mark groaned. My brain never seems to turn on little light bulbs. They're always large and blinding, like "Why don't we just hit the road?"

"Are we in this for real?" I asked. "Really and truly? Until we've given it all we've got and we grind to a total halt?"

"I thought we'd already agreed on that," said Mark. "So what's your idea?"

"Well," I said, sliding down into the water until only my face broke the surface, "If we really and truly want to find out if we can build an audience and sell advertising, we have to do some serious, big gun publicity. The evening news in Port Angeles and Calgary were lovely, but we can't rely on hit-or-miss tactics. I think we should hire a public relations firm."

Mark sat up, and so did I. I could see his brain turning over logistics behind his eyes. I'm always seized by grand visions. He's always struck with details, the Rube Goldberg machinery it takes to actually make things happen.

"I know someone who does that sort of thing," I said. "I met him at a convention where he was handling the press. I can send him e-mail and ask him some questions."

The moon set, and we climbed out of the bedrock pool. Still steaming, we walked back down the hill to the Phoenix in the darkness. The next morning, I sent an e-mail message to Gerry, who worked for a large, prestigious public relations firm in New York. We hit the road south, and even though we didn't know it, the Idaho border was our Rubicon. Now that we'd set our sights on a blitz of high-powered publicity, there was no going back.

Gerry, who was understandably concerned about the sort of budget we were likely to represent, had diplomatically offered to give us the names of less expensive free-lancers, and he even suggested ways we might handle publicity ourselves. His firm, whose clients included the Duchess of York, Kathie Lee Gifford, and any number of other celebrities and large corporations, was hardly the low-cost choice. I knew that, I replied, and that's why I'd written. We wanted to do everything in our power to propel *RoadTrip America* to marketability, I explained, and we had a window of opportunity that wouldn't stay open forever. We didn't want second best, and we'd already tried do-it-yourself. We could understand if we were too small a potato to be of interest to a firm like his, but a firm like his was what we wanted. Finally I asked simply, "Do you want the job?" The question hung in the air as we pulled into Wallace, Idaho.

"I Saw You On TV!"

Wallace was covered in volcanic ash when we arrived, an unnatural disaster caused by the filming of Dante's Peak, a high-budget movie about a volcano that blows its stack and obliterates a small town. Wallace didn't have a mountain, which in the era of digital effects is easy to fix, but it did have an adorable mining town main street and residents eager to cooperate, partly "For the Glory" and mostly "For the Money."

By the time we arrived, the glory had worn off, and business owners who hadn't been able to open their front doors for three weeks were beginning to grumble that the money wasn't worth it, either. Even so, it was clear that Wallace was having a memorable summer, and we settled into a campground next to the old railroad depot where we could hobnob with the locals, enjoy the excitement, and even borrow a telephone to download the e-mail message that sealed our fate for the next four months.

In August, we would commence a national publicity tour orchestrated by Gerry's firm. We'd start in the west and cover "major media markets" across the country. We'd wind up before Thanksgiving in New York City, the press and publishing capital of the Western world. By then, we reasoned, we'd be seasoned spokespersons for our cause, and our track record of coverage in other markets would help crack through the jaded, we've-seen-it-all veneer of Big Apple news moguls.

Our plan was going to take all we had, not just financially, but in every other respect, too. Not only would we continue to publish daily features on *RoadTrip America*, we'd be arriving in a new city each week. We'd been arriving in strange places on a near-daily basis for two years, of course, but now we'd be trolling for "hits," interviews with newspaper reporters, radio talk show hosts, and television personalities. It was a whole new, eye-opening enterprise, the unlikely coalition of two nomads in a motorhome and a team of Manhattan fame brokers.

Our first "media market" was Las Vegas, and when we arrived it would have been 110° in the shade, but there was no shade. Our thermometer read 116°, fairly normal for August. Nadine, who worked with Gerry and had been assigned to our account, had landed a "remote shoot" with the "CBS Evening News." That meant that we had to wear little speakers in our ears, look into a camera, and pretend that we could see the news anchor sitting at his cool desk in the studio. I'd seen a thousand such interviews, but let me assure you, it's different when you're the one wearing the bug. We squinted into the sun and tried to ignore the sweat pouring down our foreheads and backs. We smiled and talked, and I can't remember a word I said. It was baptism by fire.

And it worked. The casino at which we were staying was pleased to receive positive if indirect publicity, and the general manager bought us dinner. Several people recognized us as we left the dining room, and *RoadTrip America* registered an increase in traffic. By the next morning, our e-mail box was full of messages from Las Vegans who'd watched the news. Before we departed for Utah, we had also been interviewed for the *Las Vegas Sun*. Two hits. Not bad.

And so it went. We connected dots across the continent: Salt Lake City, Denver, St. Louis, Chicago, Indianapolis, Cleveland, Pittsburgh, Philadelphia, Washington, D.C. By the time we arrived in New York City, we had honed not only our public personas but an entirely new set of skills virtually unheard of in the Winnebago crowd. The majority of RV owners stay away from big cities for obvious reasons. For starters, most of them acquired motorhomes to escape urban landscapes. Places to stay are harder to find in metropolitan areas, and parking is a guaranteed nightmare. And of course, most RV owners are not on publicity tours. They're on vacation. The last thing they want to think about is washing their vehicle or parking in Times Square, but in our quest for publicity, we embraced such challenges. They were a far cry from grizzly habitats and icy mountain roads, but big cities tested our mettle just as thoroughly.

Washing the Phoenix was a weekly challenge. It needed to shine in photographs, and it was too tall for ordinary car washes. We often spent the better part of a day searching for a truck wash and waiting in line with dozens of eighteen-wheelers. If we were lucky, we'd find a do-it-yourself establishment with a tall bay, but sometimes we had to rely on the kindness of campground owners who'd loan us a hose and a bucket.

And we had to look as slick as we could, too, which meant braving the scariest thing of all about life on the road. If I asked you what's most frightening about traveling in a motorhome, you might guess guys with guns or traffic accidents, but those are way down the list. The most terrifying thing is haircuts. There was a time in my purse-and-pantyhose past that I took for granted the regular attentions of Dana Marie, a hair artiste of the first order. I trusted her completely, and even let her dye my hair if she thought it was a good idea. My head was in her hands every six weeks.

Unfortunately, there's no such thing as a virtual haircut, and for the first few months on the road, I kept putting off the inevitable day when I'd have to darken the door of an alien beauty salon. I stayed shaggy most of the time, but when we launched our publicity tour, I knew I'd have to muster my courage and start trusting my pate to strangers on a regular basis.

Celebrities always take their hairdressers on tour, and I no longer think they're spoiled. The day I looked into a mirror in Denver and stifled a scream was the day I understood Madonna. I would have gladly paid Dana Marie's expenses to meet us in St. Louis. Lacking a movie star budget, I fell back on my Stampede cowboy hat. Suddenly it became my favorite accessory.

And I wasn't the only one facing a grooming challenge. Marvin had to look good, too, now that he was a media darling. I'd long since perfected the art of bathing him in the Phoenix One's shower, but, being a fluffy sort of dog, he needed to be shorn once in a while. While I was shaking at the thought of trusting my head to an unknown clipper, Marvin had to turn his whole body over to strangers. We never knew whether he'd turn out looking like a poodle or an Airedale, but Marvin never complained.

"He's a sweetheart," the groomers always said. He was a trouper, too. He even learned to smile for cameras, except once when an overzealous interviewer thrust a microphone into his muzzle. Marvin growled on the six o'clock news, and we got e-mail asking why we traveled with "such a mean dog."

Many large cities are devoid of RV parks. This fact, while not surprising, made studio appearances on early morning television shows an interesting challenge. In Chicago, the closest place we could find to stay overnight was near Joliet, almost fifty miles from downtown. In order to shower, walk Marvin, put the truck in order, and still be on time for a five a.m. shoot, we had to get up at 2:30. "At least we aren't stuck in rush hour traffic," said Mark as we sailed into Chicago in the dark. And who would have guessed that dawn in Chicago is a wondrous thing. The sun rose over Lake Michigan, setting fire to every window, turning every surface gold. Parked on a bridge with a magnificent view, the Phoenix joined many a Chicago household for breakfast that morning on the early news. Afterwards, as we made our way slowly through the newly awakened metropolis, a man ran along the sidewalk, his face bright with a broad grin. "I saw you!" he shouted. "I saw you on TV!"

By the time we got to the east coast, our horns were no longer green. We'd faced scores of cameras and microphones, and we'd shaped and reshaped our message. *RoadTrip America* was an appealing human interest story, and if we couldn't make the grade on our own, Marvin was a proven crowd pleaser. "Sex, kids and animals," Gerry had said. "They always sell."

On October 10, 1997, we crossed New Jersey and drove over the George Washington Bridge into the Big Apple. The Phoenix was ready to take Manhattan.

· 17 ·

Quantum Leap
To New Horizons

The Phoenix Takes Manhattan

If Chicago had seemed like a daunting metropolis, Manhattan eclipsed it easily. I'd been here before and found it intimidating on foot. Now I was encased in thirty-two feet of steel, which I was sure was at least twenty-two feet too many.

But wait. Big trucks drive through New York all the time. So do buses. So what's the big deal? Mark pointed out all these truths to me, and I decided I might as well relax. At least there were no cliffs, and my job was one I was good at. I was the navigator. I'd figure out which routes the eighteen-wheelers used, and steer our course accordingly.

The trouble is, the Phoenix isn't a big rig. It's a motorhome, which means it carries propane. Propane qualifies as "hazardous material," and in New York, that puts serious limitations on where you can drive. I couldn't guide Mark along truck routes without first making sure they didn't end up at the Holland Tunnel or on the bottom level of the George Washington Bridge. To put it simply, I screamed a lot, especially when an irritatingly unavoidable Moebius strip of expressway kept dumping us onto

Jerome Avenue in the South Bronx.

With all its hubbub and legendary intensity, Manhattan was unbeatably exhilarating. Mark soon found that the Phoenix One's size was an asset. We were just large and unusual enough to make taxi drivers flinch, and in the time it took for them to recover, Mark could change lanes or turn corners. We drove to the high rise home of our publicists on Avenue of the Americas. Gerry and Nadine met us on the sidewalk in front, and we took them for a spin in the truck they'd been promoting for three months sight unseen.

"We've got MSNBC lined up," said Nadine. "They want to spend a day in the city with you, shooting a piece for a show called "The Site." We've also got reporters from *The Wall Street Journal, Newsday,* and the *Staten Island Advance* who want to interview you, a crew from First TV that wants to shoot you in Times Square, and a couple of radio interviews. Oh, and *People* magazine wants to talk to you."

People was heady news. Anything nationally distributed was good, and a magazine that has a long shelf life in doctors' offices and nail salons was even better. Of course, it wasn't a sure thing yet. We had to go to *People* headquarters first, and let them make sure we were of genuine interest to other humans.

People lives at the top of the Time-Life Building in midtown Manhattan, an area notoriously short on parking spaces. In order to keep our appointment, we parked the Phoenix One in Pleasantville and rode a commuter train into the city. My sister lives in Pleasantville, and we left the Phoenix filling her driveway. As we left, we mentioned that we'd searched everywhere, but so far we hadn't been able to discover a place to empty our holding tanks. "Don't worry," said Libby. "I'll make some phone calls."

When we returned from our pilgrimage to the Time-Life Building, Libby had exercised her considerable talent for uncovering esoteric information. She had discovered an establishment that most residents of greater New York will never have the need to know about, much less visit. She had learned the whereabouts of the Hawthorne Receiving Manhole, a public doorway to the sewers of Westchester County. "And you can use it for free," she said triumphantly.

Life in a motorhome in New York City is a study in contrast. Within two hours, we'd traveled from glamor to squalor, from *People* magazine's lofty aeries overlooking Radio City Music Hall to a public sewer.

"I can't figure out why this thing is called a manhole," commented Mark as he wrestled once again with a recalcitrant hose. "No man in his right mind would go down there."

The editors of *People* decided that *RoadTrip America* was their kind of story. They'd like to photograph us in a rural setting, they said, a backdrop suggesting autumn on the open road. It was the end of November, and the leaves were falling as fast as the temperatures.

"I don't know if there's any left," said Libby when we told her we needed fall color, "But there's only one good way to find out." We piled into her car, and two hours later, we'd found three trees that weren't yet bare and a roadside apple stand. They all looked good to us, and we figured we'd spend a couple of hours with the photographer.

We couldn't have been more inaccurate in our prediction, and I now look at the photographs in *People* with new eyes. We spent two full days with Peter and his assistant. He shot fifty rolls of film. By the time Peter's shutter closed for the last time, Marvin was ready to bite him, and Mark would have cheered if he had. My face was frozen into a smile, and my nose was numb. Nonetheless, we all look smashing in the picture that appeared the first week of December, 1996.

The story in *People* caused our "traffic" to rise sharply and continued to fill our e-mail box with messages for months. It also illustrated perfectly what I had predicted about *RoadTrip America*'s shelf life as a publicity hook. The piece about us appeared in a section called "Bytes." *People* discontinued "Bytes" less than a year later. Web sites had become mundane. They were no longer stories in their own right.

By the time *RoadTrip America*'s media blitz drew to an end, we were back in California. We finished up with a studio interview in San Francisco with C|Net, and then we headed to Pasadena, because lo and behold, it was nearly time for the Rose Parade. Mark had been tapped to be "Barn Chief" again, and once more, the Phoenix One would enjoy an exclusive Rose Bowl address for New Year's.

"We'll Go To Arizona"

I'd never understood how an operation could be successful if the patient died, but I did after we completed a post mortem on *RoadTrip America*'s publicity tour. The tour had been an unqualified media success. We'd enjoyed "hits" all over the country, and we'd capped it off with a good showing in New York. *RoadTrip America*'s audience had expanded with each piece of coverage and, even better, had retained much of its growth. We had thousands of regular readers and countless more casual visitors every day.

In spite of it all, we still couldn't put a good price on banner ads, and we hadn't hired public relations royalty and driven a five thousand-mile circuit to sell them at throw-away rates. By the time the Rose Parade had marched away down the boulevard, we knew it was time to change tacks, even though neither one of us was struck with a single notion of what to do next.

In January, 1997, the only thing Mark and I knew for sure was that we were going to continue publishing *RoadTrip America*, even if we didn't know where it would take us or how we would pay for it. More than just a Web site, *RoadTrip America* was a community, our community, a place we'd built and furnished and invited the world to visit. And the world had come. We had readers in Hungary, Croatia, Japan, Brunei Darussalam. We'd made friends from Oyster Bay, New York to Issaquah, Washington. The Web worked. *RoadTrip America* worked. Somehow we'd keep our wheels rolling. We had to. Somewhere along the highway, *RoadTrip America* had become inextricably intertwined with who we were and why we were on earth.

On January 23, 1997, we had $284 in our checking account, a full tank of gas, and a refrigerator full of food.

"What should we do?" I asked Mark for perhaps the thousandth time. I didn't expect an answer, but this time I got one.

"We'll go to Arizona," he said. Well, what the heck? There was nothing to be gained by sitting around and moping.

"We've been invited to tour the 911 dispatch center in Scottsdale," said Mark, "And we have a standing invitation to stay at Southwestern Academy, a boarding school near Sedona."

"I'd like to stop in Quartzsite," I added. "It's supposed to have the world's largest RV encampment and swap meets that never end. It'd make a great story."

The two weeks we spent in Arizona were mysterious and wonderful. They were mysterious because I know we had $284 to our name when we left, and somehow we never ran out of money. I can't explain it now, but we had enough to take two friends to dinner at an expensive restaurant. Somehow we had enough to give $100 to one of those friends, not because she asked, but because she appeared to need it. That accounts for at least $230 right there, and I know it's utterly impossible that we lived on $54 for fourteen days, especially since we were driving, and it takes more than that to fill our gas tanks. I can't explain it in any terms but these. It was miraculous. We passed out meager loaves, and when we gathered the scraps, we had more than when we started.

The stories we posted on *RoadTrip America* during those two surprising weeks remain among our most popular. We interviewed two women who had built an Earthship, an energy-efficient home built out of old tires, and a married couple who were putting the final touches on a house made out of straw bales. We arrived in Quartzsite the day a hundred antique steam engines were up and running, and we wrote a story about Diane Hall, whose doctor father had cared for Rudolph Hess when he was a prisoner of war in England during World War II. We stayed at Southwestern Academy for nearly a week, meeting students who hailed from around the globe and enjoying the school chef's excellent cooking. We taught classes on how to make Web pages, and I posted the students' handiwork on *RoadTrip America*. Marvin swam in a pond and made friends with the seven resident dogs.

And then, right out of the Arizona blue, something unexpected happened. The power of e-mail and the World Wide Web united to bring us a six-month contract with a major public relations firm in New York City.

This Truck Fueled By Nicotine

It happened like this. One day while we were staying at Southwestern Academy, we received an e-mail message from a publicist we'd met in Connecticut. He included the text of an ad he'd come across in the New York Times. Someone with a Manhattan fax number was looking for two people to drive a motorhome on a coast-to-coast publicity tour.

My immediate thought was that such a tour was likely to be sponsored by (a) a tobacco company or (b) a beer manufacturer, and I couldn't see myself driving around in a Marlboro truck or a Budweiser van. Since I didn't know for sure, I pursued the lead and soon discovered that the fax number belonged to a major public relations firm, a competitor of the one that had handled our tour. A little more sleuthing uncovered some names, and before too many days had passed, we were in serious conversations with a publicity team launching a twenty-city media tour to showcase products designed to help people quit smoking: Nicorette gum and NicoDermCQ patches. The tour's other sponsor was the American Cancer Society, and the vehicle was a 34-foot Airstream Class "A" motorhome dubbed the NicoVan.

On February 7, after negotiation by e-mail, fax and telephone, we signed a contract with the public relations firm. Although at first we had planned to fly to New York City for a face-to-face meeting, *RoadTrip America*'s presence on the Web offered enough in the way of introduction that we concluded our conversations without a personal interview.

It was fortunate we didn't have to take the time for a cross-country plane trip. The NicoVan was set to hit the road in San Francisco in less than two weeks, and we had work to do in the meantime. We had to drive to northern California, find a place to store the Phoenix One, and metamorphose ourselves into spokespersons for smoking cessation, which isn't quite anti-tobacco, but in the politically charged atmosphere of the day, we needed to be able to explain the difference.

By February 19, the Phoenix had been rusticated at a storage facility for racing boats in San Jose. Before Mark drove her there and returned by commuter train, we'd pulled her next to the NicoVan, which was parked at the Sunnyvale firm that was applying its graphics. We'd had about three hours to move our belongings from one vehicle to the other. We had to move fast, and in the rush, neither of us gave a thought to Marvin. He was sitting in the front seat of the Phoenix as we worked, his usual spot when we were stationary. It wasn't until we were almost finished that I noticed Marvin sitting in the front seat of the Nico-Van. When the center of gravity had shifted to the new vehicle, so had the dog.

By the time Mark had rushed off in the Phoenix to get to the storage yard before it closed, I was standing in a heap of bedding, clothes, kitchen utensils, tools, computers, printers and assorted office equipment. It was a surprisingly large array for people who claimed to practice minimalism, I thought, but I set about stashing it all in the NicoVan's cabinets and cupboards.

When Mark returned hours later from an exciting adventure in public transportation that had included an unintentional detour through a restricted military installation, I was pleased that I'd been able to find homes for most of our belongings. I had also come to the realization that while the Phoenix One lacked amenities that the NicoVan had in abundance, like window treatments and throw pillows and mirrored cabinets, it had been uniquely wonderful in having an office. "I did fine with kitchen stuff and clothes," I said to Mark when he finally returned. "But I have no idea where to put the fax machine."

Together with the computers and printers, the fax machine rode under the galley table for three days. On the fourth day, I discovered by accident that the mattress of the queen-sized bed in the back room rested on a hinged plywood platform. Lifted, it exposed a shallow storage cabinet as big as the bed. That unlikely space immediately became our office. When we needed to work, we took the equipment out from under the bed and set it up on the galley table, the kitchen counter, and, when both Mark and I needed to work at the same time, a separate folding table. It worked, but it underscored the fact that recreational vehicles are aptly named. They're great for playing cards and watching television, but without major remodeling, they're difficult places to get anything done.

Of course, our work for the NicoVan project took place largely outdoors. When we reached an event location, anything from a supermarket parking lot to a county fair, we'd unfurl an awning and set up four tables upon which we'd display free literature about the dangers of smoking, how to stop, and how to use Nicorette gum and NicoDermCQ patches. We'd be joined by pharmacists, sales representatives, and American Cancer Society volunteers. If our publicists were successful, we'd attract television crews and newspaper reporters, and no matter what, we'd attract a stream of people who smoked, or people who wished someone they knew would quit.

Our first big event was Chinese New Year's in San Francisco. We parked on Grant Avenue, where a million people muster every year for a festival and a parade featuring a hundred-foot dragon and non-stop firecrackers. Since the event lasted for two days, we had the pleasure and privilege of sleeping in the NicoVan in the heart of Chinatown on Chinese New Year's Eve.

We slept for exactly one hour. At the stroke of midnight, a cherry bomb exploded directly beneath us. We all screamed, even Marvin, and that was the end of slumber time. The bomb had exploded right next to the gas tank, and we weren't taking any more chances. We added "security guard" to our list of NicoVan responsibilities, and we dubbed our debut "Baptism by Firecracker."

Most venues were tamer than Grant Avenue on New Year's, of course, and within a month, Mark and I were seasoned veterans at conducting events. From San Francisco, we headed south to Los Angeles, and then began a long trek east by way of Phoenix, Dallas, Houston, New Orleans, and Atlanta. The pace was familiar, and we knew where all the truck washes were. Our own publicity tour had been the perfect apprenticeship.

A discovery we'd made while living aboard the Phoenix One was that an open door was the only kind worth having. It didn't make sense, we reasoned, to drive an intentionally intriguing vehicle without being willing to answer questions and give tours. If someone knocked on our door or stopped us in a parking lot, we always invited them inside. We always took the time to chat. In two years, we'd entertained visitors of every color, background, size and income bracket. Children, church goers, Girl Scouts, factory workers, university students, garage mechanics, hamburger chefs, golfers, pilots, cowboys, parking lot attendants, traffic cops, homeless people and beauty queens had all climbed up the steps and come inside to visit. What had seemed as though it would be a gross invasion of privacy had exactly the opposite effect. Somehow, the less we defended our turf, and the more we made strangers our welcomed guests, the less we felt invaded, and the more we felt at home no matter where we roamed.

The same policy worked well with the NicoVan. People didn't want tours, but they did want information. We talked to toll takers and gas station attendants, waitresses and traffic cops. Truckers would call us by CB radio as we rolled down the highway, and we'd pull over and give them information at the next truck stop. I'd never smoked, but I quickly came to respect the power of tobacco addiction, and how important it was to support the efforts of anyone determined to conquer it. Mark had smoked briefly when he'd served as a firefighter for the Forest Service, and his own experience with quitting added understanding and credibility to his natural talent for counseling.

Traveling in the Phoenix One, we had often struck up conversations that centered around following dreams. "If you can do this, than I can follow my own dreams of travel," said a woman we met high in the Blue Ridge Mountains of Virginia. "You give me strength." A year later, she sent us a postcard from Africa. She'd made the strength her own.

I soon realized that giving up an addiction is like pursuing a dream. To be successful, it helps to gain strength from those who've covered analogous ground. Our metaphor was different in the NicoVan, but our message was the same. You can get where you want to go. Take the first step. Ask for help when you need it. Believe. It's the recipe for gaining your heart's desire, whatever in the world that might be. It was the same recipe that had kept us on the road for over four years.

And what was happening with *RoadTrip America* all this time? Our online community was alive and well. We redesigned the site, and we posted new features weekly. *RoadTrip America* flourished as the NicoVan progressed, and we continued publishing a print newsletter called *RoadTrip Report*, the descendant of the *Phoenix One Journal*. The newsletter's mailing list had grown to over a thousand and included subscribers from around the world.

Out Of The Twister, Into The Fire

Life aboard the NicoVan became routine, but it was never boring. The publicity firm in New York worked constantly to secure press coverage, and we put our freshly honed media skills to work fielding radio interviews by telephone and setting up the

NicoVan's display in the parking lots of television studios.

In Deerborn on the second of July, we were running a standard gig in front of a supermarket. Mark was talking to a man in a business suit, but otherwise the parking lot was deserted. A thunderstorm was threatening, and, except for the three of us, everyone had taken cover inside cars and buildings.

Suddenly, a siren blared with a loud, undulating scream.

"What's that?" asked the man to whom Mark was speaking.

"It's a tornado warning," said Mark, an avid weather watcher who knows such things even though he's never lived in twister land. "But don't you know? You live here."

"I've never heard that thing in my life," said the man, eyes wide. Come to think of it, I'd never heard of tornadoes hitting Detroit, either. Didn't funnel clouds stick to Kansas and Oklahoma? Just then, the store manager burst through the doors, screaming at a bag boy who had just emerged.

"Get inside!" he bellowed. The man in the suit scurried to his car. Mark and I watched in amazement as half a dozen shopping carts began circling the parking lot on their own. Without saying a word to each other, we packed up our displays in record time. The sky had turned a strange khaki color, and the siren was still screaming as we pulled out of the parking lot.

The sky was lighter to the east, and, lacking any other information about which way to go, we decided it was as good a direction to head as any. The streets were deserted except for one pickup truck with New York license plates that was directly in front of us and moving at a snail's pace. Just as I was ready to jump out and tell the driver to sight see elsewhere, the truck turned and we picked up speed.

But so did the wind. It grew horrifyingly fierce, engulfing us in a vortex of whirling debris, leaves and branches at first, and then street signs, shingles, trash cans, slats from bus stop benches. An unspoken question hung between us. Should we park the van and run, or should we keep driving?

Suddenly and without warning, we were engulfed in a whirling torrent of rain. It obliterated our vision and turned the sky even darker. Just when we were seeing ourselves on tomorrow's list of storm victims, an underpass appeared in front of us. Two cars had already pulled to the side underneath it, but there was still room for 34 feet of NicoVan. "Phew," I said as we breathed normally for the first time in half an hour. "This came along in the NicoTime. Heh, heh."

I thought we would be able to wait under the bridge until the storm passed, but suddenly I noticed that we were sitting in a depression in which the water level was rising ominously. Unlike the Phoenix One, the NicoVan had extremely low clearance, and it wouldn't be long until we were afloat.

"I'll keep watching," I said to Mark. "I'll tell you when we have to leave." Only five minutes had passed when we joined the cars ahead of us and pulled onto higher ground to avoid being flooded. The storm had abated slightly. It was still raining, but the wind had quieted to the point at which large objects were staying on the ground. We could drive, and soon we were headed northwest on the expressway that would take us to the campground where we'd been staying. We hoped it had escaped the path of the storm, which we now realized was heading east, toward Lake St. Clair.

We passed a car that the wind had flipped like a tortoise, and we marveled at the piles of debris left in the storm's wake. Just as our shoulders were relaxing, just as we thought we'd made it through unscathed, the hail started.

Heavy hail and motorhomes are not a good combination. We'd seen the effect a good BB-shower had on a brand-new trailer in Missouri. It looked like it had been used for target practice at an Uzi school.

"Uh-oh," I said. "This could be very, very bad." But just then, another underpass materialized out of nowhere. We screeched to a fast halt underneath it, and the hailstorm soon spent all its ammunition. The sky lightened, and we drove on. Our campground was completely untouched.

Two days later, on the fourth of July, we had no NicoVan events scheduled. Early in the morning, I turned on the television to learn the latest news about the storm. The stories weren't happy. A dozen people had lost their lives, and several neighborhoods had been destroyed. The Red Cross was asking for volunteers to help clear streets and mend houses.

"We could do that," I said. "Why don't we call?" I knew Mark would like the idea. As a former Red Cross disaster specialist, it was just the sort of situation for which he'd been trained. He called, and we spent the day at a devastated mobile home park north of the city. Mark chopped down trees to clear roads, and I served refreshments from the NicoVan. That night, we watched fireworks from a hilltop near our campground. They were beautifully boring, mere child's play after the weather extravaganza of two days before.

I wish I could say that Detroit's tornado attack was the closest call we ever had aboard the NicoVan, but months later in Virginia Beach, we faced an even more frightening threat. We were driving along an expressway in the direction of the local chapter of the American Cancer Society when, BAM! I thought a tire had exploded.

Mark pulled off the road, and we leapt out to check our tires. They seemed to be intact, but a wisp of steam was escaping from under the right front wheel. I sniffed it.

"That's not steam," I said. "It's smoke."

Mark jumped back inside the vehicle and suddenly two computer cases and a cellular telephone were hurtling my way with Marvin in hot pursuit.

"Catch!" yelled Mark. "And call for help!"

The NicoVan was on fire. I could see flames leaping three feet high inside the coach. I grabbed Marvin, slid down a grassy embankment, and dialed 911.

What was I saying about haircuts and hail? Trust me, they are insignificant irritations compared to the worst threat of all. Bar none, fire is a motorhome's deadliest enemy. Nearly everything is flammable, and the parts that aren't will still vanish in a holocaust of exploding gas and propane tanks.

Thanks to Mark's skill with a fire extinguisher, the immediate intervention of a good Samaritan in a glass delivery truck, and the subsequent arrival of the Virginia Beach Fire Department, the NicoVan and its inhabitants escaped vaporization.

"You had about fifteen seconds," said one of the firemen. "Then it would have been ka-boom."

As it was, it took a week to set the NicoVan to rights. Mark, Marvin and I moved into a hotel that welcomed dogs, and a Mack truck repair shop rebuilt the NicoVan's electrical system. Miraculously, the interior of the coach had escaped damage except for a fine layer of white dust, the spent contents of two fire extinguishers.

It had taken two, and the van was equipped with one. The anonymous angel in the glass delivery truck had provided the other, then vanished before we could shake his hand. Nowadays, we always carry two red cylinders, and whenever anybody asks for road safety advice, we always say, "Buy an extra extinguisher. You may catch on fire in a place where there are no glass delivery trucks."

After the NicoVan's media tour drew to an end in St. Louis, Mark and I worked directly with its corporate sponsors to launch a second circuit. From August, 1997 to January, 1998, the Nico-Van was managed by the company we founded for the purpose. RTA Marketing was a quantum leap toward our goal of reaching the new horizons made possible by mobile communication. Technology had given us a home as wide as the continent. The virtual kingdom brought us community that circled the globe. With RTA Marketing, we entered the corporate realm.

· 18 ·

Dashboard Dreams

"You Don't Look Like You Live in a Van!"

During our second year on the road, Mark and I were invited to a dinner party at the Knickerbocker Club in Manhattan. We chatted with the other guests and exchanged the usual information about residence and profession.

Except we were distinctly unusual, conversation-stopping in fact. A silence hung in the air after Mark described the Phoenix One. I felt a dozen eyes raking me from head to toe. A regal matron in a designer dress broke the spell. "You don't look like you live in a van!" she blurted. It was perhaps the most sincere compliment I've ever been paid.

But what do people who live in vans look like if they don't look like us? The problem lay not in our appearance, but in the expectations of a race of apartment dwellers. It was funny, really. I've been in Manhattan studios that are no bigger than the Phoenix, and I'd never dreamed of saying to their occupants, "You don't look like you live in a gym locker!"

But you learn to expect ejaculations of surprise when you mix cultures in unlikely ways. You're shocking when you want to conduct business with corporate America without owning a purse, when you dine at the Knickerbocker Club only hours after a visit to the Hawthorne Receiving Manhole. When you're blazing trails, you have to learn to love the evidence that your machete is cutting through virgin brush, because most of the time, your progress is invisible to outside observers. After all, you don't look like you live in a van.

We'd had to establish a stationary office in a megalopolis in order to give RTA Marketing credibility in its first incarnation. The blanket assumption that a business of any import could not be run from mobile corporate headquarters was still too firmly entrenched in the minds of potential clients, and our solution was almost laughable. RTA Marketing was still operated from the road. It just didn't look like it lived in a van.

In the course of five years on the road, we'd hacked out solutions to many challenges facing mobile entrepreneurs, and with every improvement in our ability to conduct business and communicate, we raised our expectations a notch or two. The black box had been the first hurdle in what has become a long obstacle course toward nirvana: reliable, fast communication that works anywhere, anytime. The *deus ex machina* I once conjured to effect e-mail on the fly is now a minor demigod in a whole new tantalizing pantheon. Satellite communication looms on a near horizon.

As with all new technology, the power that satellite systems promise will be useless until we take it home like a newborn child. We'll have to nurture it and fall in love with it, let it charm us, teach us, drive us nuts with exuberant adolescence. Only when we embrace it and weave it into the fabric of our lives does technology gain the power to transform.

The transformation has already begun, quietly, without fanfare. Corporations with large fleets of service technicians are equipping their vehicles with specialized radio systems to transmit voice and data in the field. Trucking companies install e-mail systems in the cabs of big rigs. Even the ubiquity of pagers and hand-held cellular telephones is part of the revolution.

If you ask someone to name a mobile business, chances are he'll say, "Hot dog cart," "Ice cream truck," or "Carnival game." These enterprises and their cousins have been staples of fair circuits, suburban neighborhoods and boardwalks for decades. Their owners are as interested as anyone else in the advances in telecommunications, and improved systems will make their lives easier.

But what of businesses that have never been mobile, businesses that have been tethered to location by the need for communication and community, but whose operations could be carried out on the edge of Flathead Lake as easily as on Wall Street? And what of enterprises in rural areas, where scattered populations mean that professionals must travel hundreds of miles a day no matter where they set up shop? Reliable mobile communications coupled with innovative vehicle design have the power to change the face of business forever.

Mark and I had progressed from free-lance writing to journalism to online publishing, all on a roll, and we'd followed up by managing a marketing company from the road. Dashboard entrepreneurship works, and we've barely plumbed its possibilities, barely identified it as an emerging phenomenon. But emerging it is, even if it's not always obvious. Dashboard professionals can't yet afford to look like they live or work "in a van." They can't afford earning epithets like "on the lam" or "fly-by-night." In this they know a kinship with Native American hunters, the Nez Percé, the Umatillas. The agrarian history of Western Europe holds the American majority firmly in thrall. If you move around untethered to a base, you're either poor or you've got something to hide. People shouldn't be trusted unless they've got addresses supported by dirt, preferably dirt for which they hold the deed.

The most valuable real estate Mark and I own is our virtual domain on the World Wide Web. As miraculous as it still seems, it's provided us with a new vision of home, community, and business. More than once, when someone asks me where I live, I've been tempted to answer, "Cyberspace." I don't, though, because it's not quite true. As long as I still have to get real-life haircuts, I'm still living in the world of three dimensions. My permanent address may reside in the virtual universe, but at night, it's not where I lay me down.

While I have no desire to live in virtual space, I welcome the power of its metaphor. The architects of cyberspace have christened their formless constructs with comforting nomenclature imported straight from the heartland. "Home" and "mailbox" lead the list of terms that suggest sedentary permanence. It's a helpful benefit for the perennially migratory, since the bulk of English travel words carry negative connotations: migrant, vagabond, rover, transient. If you're constantly in motion, you're always having to explain yourself, but if you can point to a presence on the Web, it's almost as reassuring as owning a fireplace. The Internet bridges the gap between a desire for roots and a yen to wander, two formerly conflicting dreams that now have a chance for simultaneous expression.

And of course the reach of cyberspace extends beyond North America's shores. It circles the globe, and even extends to extraterrestrial points when it needs to. I believe it holds the power to unite earthlings everywhere. I believe it's part of the white buffalo's promise.

A Small White Miracle

The white buffalo was born on a small farm in Janesville, Wisconsin, in 1994. For many Native Americans, her birth fulfilled a sacred prophecy and heralded a new age of peace and understanding among all the people of the world. When stories of the unusual occurrence— the odds of an albino buffalo are no better than one in ten million— were reported by the press, pilgrims began arriving in Janesville to visit the calf. Hundreds came every day, and sometimes thousands.

Paul Bethe, a friend whose path crossed ours in Chicago, asked if we'd like to join him on an expedition to see the white buffalo. "I have the address of the farm," he said. "And I know how to get there."

On a morning in early November, 1995, we set out on our pilgrimage. The day was cold and gloomy, and by the time we arrived at David and Valerie Heider's farm, steady rain had begun to fall. We parked in a boggy field, dug out our rubber boots and rain slickers, and followed makeshift signs pointing in the direction of a house and barn.

"Are we all still sure we want to do this?" asked Mark as we slipped and slid our way up the path. There was something absurd about slogging through a mire in the rain for the privilege of seeing a buffalo's child.

"We don't have to stay long," I said, "But we've come this far. It would be silly not to walk the last hundred yards." Nearby, two women and a man were carrying on a similar discussion. I heard the man say, "Shit. I can't believe I'm walking through the mud to see a damn buffalo," but none of us turned back. We soon arrived at the fence behind which Miracle was standing. Miracle. That was her name, and she was just standing there, nestled against her mother, in the rain.

People were standing nearby, a dozen or so. They were silent, and we stopped talking, too, even the swearing grumbler. My eyes were drawn to the fence. Hanging from every wire and post were offerings: tobacco pouches, feathers, handwritten messages, photographs, strands of beads.

I drew near the fence to take a closer look at Miracle, and found myself standing next to two teenage girls. One of them was crying silently. Mark and Paul joined me, and for twenty minutes or so, we just stood there in the rain.

And so did the buffalo. Nothing else happened, no sudden sun, no rainbow. We walked back to the Phoenix in the same gloomy rain, and the storm lasted far into the night.

It would be easy to dismiss the white buffalo as nothing more than a genetic freak, and a disappointing one at that. By the time we saw her, she wasn't even white any more, just noticeably lighter than her near-black relatives. But I couldn't disregard Miracle when I saw her, and I can't forget her now. The prophecy is too lovely, its incarnation too wonderful to ignore.

Miracle's presence on earth is just that, a presence. She is nothing more and nothing less than a white buffalo, a rare gift. She's artistic talent in a baby, a novel in the mind of an aspiring writer, the promise of peace among all people. She's unrequited potential, which is nothing at all unless we do our part.

The world isn't made a better place because we wish it so, but because we create it so. A path is nothing unless it's taken. Roads are merely pavement without travelers upon them. New technologies stand waiting behind a fence already festooned in offerings, but homage is only the beginning. We've paid our respects to the miracle, but unless we accept its promise and seize the day, we will find ourselves standing forever in the mud, forever wishing in the rain.

I say, what better time than now to grab your arrowhead and your red underwear? I say, let's hit the road.

Megan Edwards
At home, at work & on the road
September, 1998

Readers can visit *RoadTrip America* on the World Wide Web at:
http://www.roadtripamerica.com
RoadTrip America includes photographs of a number of the people and events described in this book and also provides current information about new developments in wireless communication.
The author can be contacted at the following e-mail address:
megan@roadtripamerica.com